SHAPEDOWN®

Just for Kids!

Level 2

Balboa Publishing · San Anselmo, CA

The development of SHAPEDOWN was supported in part by the Department of Family and Community Medicine and the John Tung/American Cancer Society Clinical Nutrition Education Center, School of Medicine, University of California, San Francisco. Developmental testing was facilitated by the Department of Pediatrics of the University. The initial development of the SHAPEDOWN Program was facilitated by the Bureau of Maternal and Child Health Services and the Division of Adolescent Medicine, University of California, San Francisco.

Use of SHAPEDOWN materials is recommended in conjunction with guidance provided by trained health/education professionals following the SHAPEDOWN Instructor's Guide.

Reviewers are requested to obtain complete program materials from Balboa Publishing at the address listed below.

© 2003 Balboa Publishing Corporation.

Fifth Edition, Revised 2003

8 7 6 5 4 3 2

Library of Congress
Cataloging in Publication Data
Mellin, Laurel M.

SHAPEDOWN Just For Kids! Level Two Workbook

Library of Congress Catalog Card No.: 88-70316
ISBN 0-935902-20-1 Paperback

Illustrations: Martha Weston
Graphic Design: Nielsen Graphics
Typography: ProType Graphics, Inc.

Published by:

Balboa Publishing Corporation
MYBOOK DIVISION
1323 San Anselmo Avenue
San Anselmo, CA 94960-2244
TEL: 415.453.8886
FAX: 415.453.8888
EMAIL: shapedown@aol.com
WEBSITE: www.shapedown.com

CONTENTS

WELCOME TO SHAPEDOWN!

Hello and welcome to SHAPEDOWN! SHAPEDOWN will help you lose weight and feel stronger and happier. It will help your family eat better food, exercise more and feel closer.

Besides food and exercise, SHAPEDOWN will teach you how to listen to your feelings and to tell people what you feel and need. When you tell your parents your true feelings, they can help you even more. You don't feel alone as much. You feel more important. TV and food become less important and it is easier to eat less and move around more.

Congratulations! Your family is special for being in SHAPEDOWN. Most kids don't go to SHAPEDOWN. They don't know about SHAPEDOWN. Your family cares so much about you that they will change their eating and exercise with you. They are special and so are you. If you like SHAPEDOWN, tell other people about it, so that other kids can get healthier, too.

How does SHAPEDOWN work? In three steps. The first step is to meet your SHAPEDOWN teacher with your parents. He or she will talk with you and your parents and give you all some important information. First, are you really too heavy? If so, how much? Second, does the extra weight hurt your health or how you feel about yourself? Your SHAPEDOWN teacher will also give you ideas about the things that may have caused you to be heavier than some of the other kids.

The second step is SHAPEDOWN. It teaches you about your food, your exercise and how to listen to your feelings. In SHAPEDOWN, you get practice in telling people how you feel and what you need. You find out how to weigh less and how to be healthier. Your parents learn the same things. The last step is ADVANCED SHAPEDOWN. In ADVANCED SHAPEDOWN, you and your parents get even more help with your weight and so that you will keep on being healthier and happier.

Have fun with SHAPEDOWN! I hope you will be able to wave goodbye to too much weight and grow up liking the size of your body. You don't have to be like those people who eat too little on diets and then later eat too much and stay heavier. You can have a body that is just the right size for you and not eat too little or too much. Then you will have more energy to become a television star, a ballet dancer, a baseball player, or whatever your dream is!

1. CINDY AND THE CLOWN'S SURPRISE

In the back of Ms. Bacon's classroom was a cozy corner. Kids lucky enough to have their desks in that corner of room 6 were out of earshot of Ms. Bacon. These four kids could whisper, tell riddles and giggle without Ms. Bacon hearing a sound. It was the middle of the year now and they were quite experienced at carefully slipping a note – with a special secret scribble in code – from desk to desk until it reached the boy or girl whose name was carefully lettered on it.

This morning Ms. Bacon had a terrible headache that she got from worrying about her bird, Meredith, who was expecting baby birds any

moment. You see, Meredith had been sitting on those eggs for so many days that Ms. Bacon was afraid that they were empty. Today she had to take the eggs to the vet to find out whether the five eggs were baby birds . . . or not.

Ms. Bacon wanted peace and quiet to nurse her headache and think about her bird. With her eyes squinting and her voice slightly shrill, she instructed the students to work for two hours straight in their math books. Two hours straight! So, the four lucky children in the cozy corner in room 6 boldly passed notes and freely giggled between math problems.

1

1

Cindy's desk was at the south side of the cozy corner, right next to the back blackboard. It was so close to the blackboard that when she came home from school most days her grandfather would say, "Now Cindy, your back is so striped with chalk that you look like a very round zebra." At that Grandfather would throw back his head and laugh until his belly shook and tears streamed down the creases in his cheeks.

Cindy would stiffen, plant a scowl on her face, stomp off to the kitchen, flip on the television and plop onto the hard wooden chair next to the cookie jar. Without fail, a round warm voice would softly call out her name again and again. The sound floated up lazily from the cookie jar clown that lived on the counter next to the hard wooden chair.

Being a very obedient girl, Cindy usually answered the round warm voice floating up from the cookie jar clown by reaching up with one hand and gently lifting off the clown's head, careful not to make a single sound. With her other hand, she would reach deep into the clown's tummy to find a bumpy round chocolate chip cookie.

But after school on the day of Ms. Bacon's headache, in March when the fragrance of apple blossoms drifted through the open window, this same round warm voice said something else. As Cindy quietly began to lift off the clown cookie jar's head, it very softly and lovingly said, "Enough is enough," and spun his head around to close the cookie jar tightly.

Cindy jumped back from the chair, her eyes round—as if she'd seen a ghost. It really was the clown cookie jar that spoke. She wasn't imagining it after all. "Enough is enough. Enough is enough? What do you mean?" Cindy muttered, still astonished. The clown hopped down from the counter and tripped over his shoes, turned to face Cindy and smiled broadly.

"Okay, Clown, you are real, but," said Cindy, her eyes narrowing, "where is my cookie? I want my cookie and I want it now!"

"There are no cookies today," replied Clown. "Do you see how empty my suit is? It's just a bag of cloth. I'm too skinny. I'm tired of giving up my cookies to you and only getting skinnier. You're fluffy, soft and round. Could we trade some of your extra fat for some of my extra lean?"

"No way, my friendly clown. I like being round and big. That way if someone doesn't share their lunch with me I can sit on them," Cindy said, and then she blushed.

"Yes, you probably sit on three or four people per day," replied Clown, smirking.

"No, not really. I mean I don't really do that . . . but sometimes I feel like doing that!" continued Cindy.

"That's okay. There are other good reasons to be round. I bet you stay warmer in winter with that extra padding. It must be wonderful to be fluffy, soft and round," sighed Clown.

"Yes, you're right, sort of. But if I think very hard I bet I could find some reasons being round is not very wonderful. For instance, last summer when my mom and I went to visit Aunt Marie in Minneapolis I was sick from the heat. Extra fat makes you feel like you're wearing a fur coat in the middle of a sauna bath."

"You could fan yourself, my sweet Cindy. I'll bet you the top yarn ball from my suit that you can't think of a single way that fat holds you back," said Clown with his round warm voice mixing with the fragrance of the apple blossoms.

"Yes, I can! Just watch me," said Cindy with a twinkle in her eye. "Of all the kids in the class I can do the least number of sit-ups."

"Nonsense," snorted Clown.

"It's not nonsense! How would you like always being the slowest and being chosen for teams the very, very last every single time?"

"There are worse things, my dear, like forgetting your homework two days in a row or having to clean under your bed," retorted Clown. "I'm not convinced."

"Wait, I have another reason, a good one. All the kids, except of course, my three friends in the cozy corner of room 6, call me names like tub-o

and they snicker and laugh when I go by."

"In my book, Cindy, that's a minor league problem. In fact, it's normal." replied Clown hopping back up onto the counter in case Grandpa came in. "Every single one of the clown cookie jars sitting on the shelf in the Rainbow China Company in Shanghai is teased for something. Some for having their red noses painted on their chins by mistake. Others for having chips of paint gone. And still others for being too tall, too short, too wide, too narrow, too soft, too hard, too cracked or too chipped. Being teased is a fact of life at the Rainbow China Company. Why should it be any different in Ms. Bacon's class?"

Cindy sighed. Would she ever convince

1

Clown? She scratched her head and her mind wandered to the math problems she had to finish by the next morning. No, she wasn't giving up, "Wait a minute, Clown. I've got a reason!" Cindy said. "Clothes! I can never find great style clothes in my size. How can I take ballet lessons without a leotard that fits?"

Clown reached over to Cindy, putting his arm around her neck and patting her on the shoulder. Then, slowly, Clown shook his head and smiled, "Cindy, your body is round and fluffy. It keeps you warm and makes you feel safe. Anyone can sew stylish clothes in any size at all. They can even sew leotards. It's simple."

"Clown!" said Cindy pulling away, her eyes flashing with anger, "What do you know about being round? It makes me feel safe sometimes, but most times it makes me feel slow and ugly and unlovable. So there!" said Cindy bursting into tears.

Clown looked down at the table. He looked up at the kitchen clock. He gazed at the kitchen counter where the bread crumbs and glob of blueberry jelly still remained from the morning's toast. A big round tear brimmed over his eyelid, rolled down his cheek and dropped onto the kitchen table. It made a bead of wetness on the newly-waxed surface.

Cindy tried to take her mind off feeling wretched and sad. She thought about the glazed, chocolate and white doughnuts with red and green sprinkles on top she had seen on television. She thought about the juicy double cheeseburgers and the crispy fries that left her fingers glistening with grease. And she thought about the round, bumpy chocolate chip cookies in the cookie jar. Suddenly, she wanted one. No, she wanted five. "Oh," said Cindy, astonished, "I know a good thing about being round. You get to eat a lot of cookies. And the cookies block out

my bad feelings. They make me feel better."

Cindy imagined her whole life, day after day, when boredom, sadness or loneliness struck, heading straight for the cookie jar. She thought about not keeping up in P.E. and incessantly thinking about food. She thought of the stomachaches after eating the tenth cookie. It was no fun.

Cindy heard her grandpa shoo the cat off the top of the piano and then bang the screen door on his way out to water the tulips and daffodils in the garden out back. Soon Mom would be home.

At last she crouched down next to the kitchen table so that her dark brown eyes gazed directly into Clown's china blue eyes and said, "I want to lose weight because enough is enough."

The clown quietly nodded. He understood. For a moment the two listened to the sound of the teakettle gently whistling on the stove, ready to make a perfect cup of tea to soothe Grandpa in the late afternoon.

Suddenly the clown's face turned stormy, "Yes, but what about me? I'm skin and bones. I don't think I'll ever get bigger, Cindy. My mother who stores the shortbread biscuits for an English lawyer in Boston and my father who keeps graham crackers for a policeman in Florida are hopelessly skinny. I will be too, no matter what I do."

"Perhaps. You're built like your Mom and Dad. And I'm built like mine. My mom is pretty round and when I went to visit my dad at Christmas, he was more than a little chunky. I figure I'll never look like a broomstick. I'll always be a little bit round—but not as round as I am now. You're built like your skinny parents, so you'll probably always be a little on the scrawny side."

Clown thought, shifting his weight from one foot to another, and then sighed. "So I'll always be a little scrawny. Isn't there anything I can do?"

"Sure," replied Cindy, "I just know I can get rid of a lot of my extra fat. If I can get rid of it, well, there's no reason why you can't get more muscle, and a little fat, too. You can get healthy just like I'm going to do. How can you expect to look healthy and grow well on a diet of straight cookies? How can you grow strong muscles when you sit on the counter all day?"

"But Cindy, how will I remember? I'm so busy keeping these cookies fresh and crisp all day that it's easy to forget about eating and exercising."

"I know, Clown. You can set goals each week, like trying to exercise for an hour each day or trying to eat only fruits and veggies for snacks. You can keep track of how many times you really stick with by using GIVE ME STROKES. I got them this week when I joined SHAPEDOWN. The SHAPEDOWN CLUB is for kids who are getting in shape. Do you like stickers?"

Clown smiled, "You bet, everywhere but on my clown suit. The glue sticks to me and no one bothers to wash it off."

"My mom and grandpa give me a sticker or some other kind of privilege like watching my favorite television program, helping me with my needle work, or, on a weekend night, letting me stay up an hour later. They give me a reward when we all make our goals for getting healthy. Plus they are so proud of me. And I'm proud of myself. I've decided to lose six pounds in the next ten weeks, to stop eating sweets when I'm bored or sad and to get in shape by walking, bouncing and dancing. You can do it, too, Clown!"

Clown smiled. . . . and winked at Cindy. He could picture himself looking healthier and stronger already. His mother who stores the shortbread biscuits for the English lawyer in Boston and his father who keeps graham crackers for a policeman in Florida had taught him a lot about food and exercise. He just hadn't put all that wisdom into practice—until now! Clown liked the idea of helping Cindy and her friends with SHAPEDOWN while he was getting healthier himself.

With that Clown folded his legs and sat on the counter as still as a cookie jar and Cindy patted him on the cap. Then she ran out the door to plant some carrot seeds in her back garden next to the tulips and the daffodils.

1

   Someone has told you that you are too fat. Maybe they're right, maybe they aren't. What you think is important. This week you will take a good look at your body and decide for yourself if you're too fat.

   Even if you are too fat, you may not want to do anything about it right now. Perhaps there are lots of reasons why you don't want to lose weight, like not wanting to cut down on cookies or not wanting to watch less television. On the other hand, there may be reasons why you want to lose weight, like so that the kids will stop teasing you, so that you that can move faster in sports or so that you feel better about yourself.

   Think about why you do want to lose weight and why you don't, then decide if you want to lose weight. If you do, SHAPEDOWN will help you make it happen. Keep in mind that even if your parents want you to lose weight, it will only happen if you make you own decision to lose weight.

   Why am I heavy? My friend, have you every wondered why you were heavy. Let me tell you a secret. You're not heavy because you did something wrong. It is not your fault. Most times there are lots of little reasons why some people are heavier than others. Can you pick out the reasons that you think you are fluffy, soft and round?

   Round genes — Round genes make your body want to be round. You get them from your parents. Just like your face looks sort of like your mother or father's face, your body may be the same shape as their's, too. If you have round genes, your body doesn't have to be really round. If you eat well and exercise a lot your body will probably be only a little bit round.

   Eating — Skipping meals, eating lots and lots of food and eating mainly HEAVY FOODS and JUNK FOODS can make your body round.

   Being Active — Sitting rather than moving around adds fat to your body. So can being bored and watching a lot of television.

   Feelings — Feeling sad, lonely, bored or worried can make you eat more. So can feeling like you're not getting the love and attention you need.

   Knowing — If you don't know how to eat a healthy diet and exercise it's hard to lose weight.

   Family — If your family likes to eat a lot of HEAVY FOODS and JUNK FOODS and doesn't like to exercise you have probably learned to act like they do. Acting like that makes most people gain weight. If your parents have a difficult time saying "no" to you, or helping you feel safe, you may exercise less or eat more.

Other kids — If your friends eat a lot of cookies and candy and offer them to you, you probably eat more. Being teased about weight makes you sad. When you're sad you may eat more.

School — If you're having trouble in school, you're probably upset about it. Feeling upset can trigger you to eat more. Also some schools have lunches and snacks that are mainly HEAVY FOODS and JUNK FOODS.

What is SHAPEDOWN like? There are no shots, pills, fake food, liquid formulas or starvation meal plans. Joining SHAPEDOWN does not mean dieting. Diets don't work. It means each week changing a little bit about your food and a little bit about your exercise. Little changes are things such as having two cookies not six, walking a mile to school rather than getting a ride and eating half a plate of vegetables at dinner. All these little changes add up to a healthy way of living - and to losing weight.

In SHAPEDOWN, the whole family joins. You are not alone in making changes. The whole family starts eating lighter - less fatty food, less sugar - and the whole family starts moving -whether it's on the bike path or on the soccer field. If your skinny sister eats chips it's not good for her either.

If you make these changes each week about a pound of extra fat will come off your body each week. Why not more? Because it can hurt your body - by robbing it of muscle rather than fat, decrease your growth and not giving you enough vitamins and minerals. Plus to lose more weight per week you have to nearly starve yourself. That makes you grouchy. It makes you feel deprived of food. We do not want you to feel deprived. We want you to enjoy food and your life now more than ever!

Often these reasons are like dominoes lined up. When one falls it knocks over the next one. For instance, Jason's parents were fighting. That made Jason worried. To block out the feelings of worry he ate more. When he ate more he gained weight and didn't feel like exercising, so he watched more television. Soon he was in the habit of eating chips, watching television and not seeing his friends after school. That just made him gain more weight. So Jason's dominoes that led to his gaining weight were: parent's troubles, feeling worried, eating high fat foods, watching television, not exercising, stopping seeing friends.

Think about the dominoes that help put weight on you! Figuring out your own dominoes makes it easier to lose weight. You know what has caused your weight. Everything — except round genes — can be changed. Even round genes really don't make you heavy. They make the difference between being slightly rounded and looking like a broomstick, that's all.

1

YOUR TURN!

Cindy thinks that she is too fat. She has lots of reasons for losing weight and for not losing weight. She has decided she wants to lose weight.

Think about yourself as you answer these questions:

1. Take your clothes off somewhere private and look at your body carefully with a full length mirror. Name three things you like about your body (for example your eyes, your legs, your hands, your ears, your nose or your shoulders):

    1. _____

    2. _____

    3. _____

2. How fat do you think your body is?

    _____ about right   _____ some extra fat

    _____ a little extra fat   _____ lots of extra fat

3. The reasons I want to lose weight (check all that are true for you):

    _____ so that I can run and move faster

    _____ so that I'll be better at sports

    _____ so that I can fit into clothes I like

    _____ so that other kids will stop teasing

    _____ so that other kids will like me better

    _____ so that my parents will be even prouder of me

    _____ so that I will be even prouder of myself

    _____ so that _____ .

4. The reasons I do not want to lose weight (check all that are true for you):

_____ because I really like sweets like cookies and candy and don't want to eat fewer of them.

_____ because I really like greasy, fatty foods like chips, butter and cheese and don't want to eat less of them.

_____ because I really like television and don't want limit it to one hour per day.

_____ because I don't want to do more exercise like walking, biking, and playing soccer.

_____ because I am used to my body the way it is and changing it is scary.

_____ because: _____

5. Do I want to lose weight?

_____ yes

_____ no

_____ not sure

6. I think that the things that helped me gain extra fat are (check all that are true for you):

_____ round genes - people in may family are heavy

_____ eating lots and lots of food

_____ skipping meals

_____ eating mainly HEAVY FOODS or JUNK FOODS

_____ sitting rather than moving around and playing sports

_____ feeling bored or not being busy enough

_____ watching more than one hour of television per day

_____ feeling sad, lonely, or worried

_____ not knowing how to eat and exercise to lose weight

_____ my parent or family having troubles

_____ my mother has a hard time saying "no" and making it stick

_____ my father has a hard time saying "no" and making it stick

_____ my mother has a hard time making me feel safe and loved

_____ my father has a hard time making me feel safe and loved

_____ my family eats a lot

_____ my family doesn't eat breakfast, lunch and dinner

_____ my family eats a lot of HEAVY FOODS and JUNK FOODS

_____ my family doesn't exercise much

_____ my family gets their fun from food not from activities

_____ my friends offer me JUNK FOODS

_____ other kids tease me about weight

_____ school is hard for me

_____ they serve HEAVY FOODS and JUNK FOODS at school or church

_____ other things _____

— GIVE ME STROKES —

Each week you will use GIVE ME STROKES. It lists some goals - some things to do each week to make you healthier and to help you lose weight. Your parent has a PARENT STROKES with the same goals on it. Both you and your parent will keep track of what you do each week on your STROKES records. Then, at the end of the week, you will add up how many days you did each thing - like how many hours of television you watched - and see if you met your goal. Let's talk about each of your goals for this week:

We took FAMILY TIME each day to look at our records and to praise each other. Your parents need your encouragement, praise and help. You need their's. Sit down with your parent once each day and take FAMILY TIME to look at each other's STROKES records and to say good things about what each of you has done.

I watched no more than 0, 2, 4, 6, or 8 hours of TV.
Watching too much TV can make you heavy. Why? Who knows? It could be because people sit down when they watch TV. Or maybe its the food people eat when they watch it. Perhaps it has to do with being alone and lonely when watching television or all the commercials of skinny people eating junk food. The number of hours you watch is up to you to choose - anywhere from 1 to 8. That's probably less than you are watching now. You should have some extra time to do other things. Go outside and play, do a project around your home, play a game with a friend, just get busy!

I EXERCISED for 50, 100, 200, 300, 400 minutes or more. Think of your poor body, starved of activity, crying to get moving. Your body craves exercise! This week you will begin giving your body what it wants. Moving around more will help your body be healthier. Your muscles will grow stronger. Exercise will help you lose weight, too. We recommend that you start off with about a half hour per day, that is, 200 minutes per week. **Any activity you do during school hours does not count.** Within a few weeks you should be exercising an hour or more per day. If you haven't been exercising much, start with walking. Later on you will design a whole exercise program for yourself.

GOAL OF THE WEEK. Each week you will have a different GOAL OF THE WEEK to work on. Your parent will have the same goal, so you can both work on it together. Often these goals are fun, things like playing a game together, having dinner together or going for a family walk. You and your parent set how many days in the week you will do it.

What about food? Eat in a healthy way this week. Next week you will learn about the MY FOOD! records and begin writing down what you eat. For now, just get used to this GIVE ME STROKES record and to starting on SHAPEDOWN.

Weight - Each week you will weigh yourself. Why? Because when you weigh yourself, you learn about your habits. Losing 1/2 to 1 pound per week is just right. If you lose more than a pound per week, you know that you are exercising too much or eating too little. If you lose less than 1/2 pound, you know that you need to change your eating and exercise more!

What does SHAPEDOWN expect from me? Quite a bit. We expect you to come to the meetings each week, even if something else comes up like play practice or your aunt's birthday. SHAPEDOWN has to come first. We expect you to read your book and to fill out your practices and quizzes. Each day, we expect you to fill in your GIVE ME STROKES record and to take FAMILY TIME. We count on you and your parent (if your parent is overweight) to lose 1/2 to 1 pound per week. If both you and your parent do these things, you will each get a reward. If even one of you does not do all these things, none of you get a reward. Each week you fill out a SHAPEDOWN Family Contract in your parent's book that says these things.

Anything else? Yes. Unless you and your parents come to the session with your SHAPEDOWN books in hand and all your practices, quizzes and records completed, none of you will be able to attend that session. Why? Because in the SHAPEDOWN session you will be using all these materials. You really can't participate well if you don't have your work done. And it's not fair to the others who have come prepared to the meeting. So if you forget your book and your parents remember to bring their's, all of you will not be able to attend the meeting. If you finish your practices but your parent does not, then neither of you will be able to attend the session.

GIVE ME STROKES

	MON.	TUES.	WED.	THURS.	FRI.	SAT.	SUN.	TOTAL	MET MY GOAL?
We took FAMILY TIME each day to look at our records and to praise each other.	✓	✓	✓	✓	✓	✓	✓	7 days	(YES) NO
I watched no more than 0 2 4 ⑥ 8 hours of TV[1].	½	½	½	½	0	3	1	6 hours	(YES) NO
I EXERCISED[2] for 50 100 ⑳⓪ 300 400 minutes or more.[3]	bike 20	soccer 60	walk 30	0	walk 40	soccer 60	swim 20	230 minutes	(YES) NO
GOAL OF THE WEEK: Our family ate dinner together on __5__ or more days.	✓	✓	✓		✓		✓	5 days	(YES) NO

TOTAL NUMBER OF GOALS MET ⇒ 4

[1] Hours per week of television:
   0 = TV STAR 2 = NEWS ANCHOR 4 = GAME SHOW HOST 6 = WEATHER PERSON 8 = GAME SHOW RUNNER UP

[2] Minutes per week of exercise:
   400 = STAR ATHLETE, 300 = IN SHAPE, 200 = GETTING STRONGER, 100 = GREAT START, 50 = GOOD TRY

[3] Get your physician's approval before exercising. If you are not now exercising, we suggest walking. Later in the program you will develop a more complete exercise program for yourself.

GIVE ME STROKES #1

	MON.	TUES.	WED.	THURS.	FRI.	SAT.	SUN.	TOTAL	MET MY GOAL?
We took FAMILY TIME each day to look at our records and to praise each other.								_____ days	YES NO
I watched no more than 0 2 4 6 8 hours of TV[1].								_____ hours	YES NO
I EXERCISED[2] for 50 100 200 300 400 minutes or more.[3]								_____ minutes	YES NO
GOAL OF THE WEEK: Our family ate dinner together on _____ or more days.								_____ days	YES NO

TOTAL NUMBER OF GOALS MET ⇒

[1] Hours per week of television:
0 = TV STAR 2 = NEWS ANCHOR 4 = GAME SHOW HOST 6 = WEATHER PERSON 8 = GAME SHOW RUNNER UP

[2] Minutes per week of exercise:
400 = STAR ATHLETE, 300 = IN SHAPE, 200 = GETTING STRONGER, 100 = GREAT START, 50 = GOOD TRY

[3] Get your physician's approval before exercising. If you are not now exercising, we suggest walking. Later in the program you will develop a more complete exercise program for yourself.

13

1

Just for Fun!

FEELINGS ABOUT WEIGHT

You probably have lots of different feelings about your weight. Some feel good; others don't. It is OK to feel lots of different feelings at once. Cindy feels sad about her weight, but her weight also makes her feel safe. Her parents are overweight, so being overweight makes her feel loyal to her family. Matt's weight makes him feel slow and bad sometimes. Other times his weight feels soft and cozy.

None of these feelings are wrong. It is important for you to know what feelings you have. Below is a list of feelings people have about being heavy. Please circle each of the feelings you have about your weight.

MY WEIGHT MAKES ME FEEL:

happy	sad	angry	safe
afraid	lonely	important	soft
not important	powerful	helpless	cozy
ugly	beautiful	wrong	good
bad	comfortable	uncomfortable	frustrated
slow	fast	like others	different
liked	not liked	friendly	not friendly

Some of these feelings feel bad. It is no fun feeling slow or wrong. The reasons you feel them is because you live in a place that thinks thin is good and fat is bad. If you lived in another country, one in which overweight was seen as good, you wouldn't have these bad feelings.

It is important to get rid of these bad feelings and to love and like your body just the way it is right now - even with the extra fat on it. Love your body. Love yourself. Lose weight out of love for yourself. I want you to love yourself and your body so much that you want to get even healthier and happier. That's what SHAPEDOWN will help you do.

How do you let go of bad feelings? Feel them. Talk about them to people who love you. Write about your feelings in a journal. Think or pray about the feelings. Later in SHAPEDOWN, we'll help you more to love your body just the way it is and to chase away bad feelings about your weight.

Directions: After you have read chapter 1, answer this practice quiz. Check your answers below. Then complete the final quiz. At your next session, you will check the answers to the final quiz.

TRUE OR FALSE

PRACTICE

____ 1. If I bring my book to the SHAPEDOWN meeting but my parent does not, I can still attend the session.

____ 2. In SHAPEDOWN, I should lose an average of 2 to 4 pounds per week.

____ 3. If one week my parent makes his or her goals and I don't, I still get a reward.

____ 4. Often when children tell their parents the absolute and complete truth about their feelings, their big appetites for television and food go away.

____ 5. We should take FAMILY TIME to praise each other's progress each day.

━━ FINAL ━━

____ 1. Parents need to keep a PARENT STROKE record even if they are not overweight.

____ 2. If I do not bring my book to a SHAPEDOWN meeting, my parents and I cannot attend it.

____ 3. To get a reward, the parents and child must meet all of their goals.

____ 4. A child's overweight can be caused by watching too much television.

____ 5. In SHAPEDOWN, I should lose an average of 1/2 to 1 pound per week.

Practice Quiz Answers: 1.F 2.F 3.F 4.T 5.T

2. MATT AND THE PIZZA PARTY

2

The very next day at school Ms. Bacon told them that the baby birds were born at the vet's. Her headache had disappeared, too. "Could headaches make baby birds crack their shells and join the world?" asked Ms. Bacon. With the dark circles under her eyes and the furrow in her brow gone, her chocolate brown eyes danced and her mouth curled into a mischievous grin.

The kids in the cozy corner giggled. Cindy chuckled. Amy and Jesse laughed. Matt leaned forward in his chair and pinched Cindy's arm. She turned and playfully slapped his hand.

The kids in the cozy corner were excited because today was their class party. Ms. Bacon's class had sold more pizzas than any other class in the whole school. They had sold pizzas to the postal carriers, fire fighters, and police officers. They had collected pizza orders from their aunts, uncles, cousins, and grandparents. Jesse had even sold a pizza to his neighbor, for his birthday present.

The students in Ms. Bacon's class had sold enough pizza to buy a new backstop for the baseball field. And now their reward—a pizza and ice cream party.

16

There was only one problem. Ms. Bacon, who frequently forgets announcements when she has headaches, forgot to tell the children about the party. So all of the kids had their regular lunches, too.

Cindy fussed to herself. Eat two lunches? She'd looked over at Matt. He was quiet. Even when he laughed, he laughed very quietly. Matt was a jock, at least he looked like one since he usually wore a football jersey. He was also heavy. Matt was big all over, like Cindy.

Should Cindy ask Matt what to do about lunch? Would he be embarrassed? He had just joined her SHAPEDOWN CLUB, too.

Cindy decided to keep quiet and to watch. She'd watch what Matt did with his lunch. For that matter, she'd keep an eye on Amy and Jesse, too. Neither of them was heavy. Maybe they had the answer.

At that very moment the bell rang so loudly that Cindy jumped. She plugged her ears with her fingers. Matt, Jesse and Amy raced to the door, grabbed their backpacks and raced for the school library. Cindy ran to catch up with them.

In the library on top of the bookshelves were tray upon tray of pepperoni pizza and vegetable pizza, and behind the pizza were 20-gallon containers of rocky road, strawberry and fudge vanilla ice cream, ready for scooping.

Within a split second all of the kids were surrounded by more pizza and ice cream than a person could exercise off in three lifetimes of dancing to MTV, 40 years of running marathons and 800 miles of bike riding.

Just as Cindy was about to eat an entire piece of pepperoni pizza in one very large bite, she stopped, sat back in her chair and played detec-tive. Cindy gazed around the room and caught sight of Jesse and Amy. They each had pieces of vegetable pizza on their paper plates and were slowly munching on them. A scoop of straw-berry ice cream was perched on the edge of Amy's plate and a scoop of rocky road on Jesse's. Their lunch bags were half open, with an apple sticking out of Amy's and a green pear on top of Jesse's.

Then she saw Matt. At once her eyes were glued to him. She stared as he stuffed in his mouth bite after bite from one, two, three, four . . . five whole pieces of pepperoni pizza. Around him kids were flying airplanes, jumping up and down and wrestling, but he noticed none of it. All he could think about was getting enough food, eating the pizza and feeling it roll around his tongue and bump its way down his throat.

Suddenly, Matt bounced up from his seat and tore over to where the librarian, Ms. Cakeland, was scooping from 20-gallon containers of rocky road, strawberry and fudge vanilla ice cream. A little river of melted strawberry ice cream ran down her arm and dripped from her elbow. Her hands were caked with sticky ice cream and her hands were ribboned with brown, pink and white goo. In a hushed voice Matt said, "I've been on a diet for two weeks. I'm going to starve right on the spot unless you give me six scoops of ice cream right this minute!" Ms. Cakeland's eyes widened and in an equally hushed voice, she said, "Why of course, Matt, growing boys must eat!" And with that she piled two scoops of rocky road, two of strawberry and two of vanilla fudge onto his plate on top of the crumbs of pizza crust and scraps of pepperoni. Matt smiled and returned to his seat, not knowing that Cindy had watched him each moment.

Cindy pushed away her pepperoni pizza and opened her lunch bag. She brought out her lunch: carrots, celery and broccoli — her ticket to

2

getting lean. Just as she was biting into a very tender carrot, she caught a glimpse of Clown sitting on Matt's shoulder.

Clown leaned back, smiled and said, "Not so smart, my fluffy, soft, round friend. Matt starved himself eating nothing but vegetables for two weeks and look at him now—stuffing himself, chowing down, pigging out, and binge eating. Starving and depriving makes you binge; binge-ing makes you fat. Is that what you want for yourself, Cindy, starving and stuffing?

Cindy pulled back from the table and said angrily, "Clown, what are you doing here at school? This is my own turf. Your place is in the kitchen. And besides, Matt will see you!"

Clown just smiled. His face began to fade. His arms and legs and hat faded and only his smile, a very broad, knowing smile remained. In a flash it disappeared, too.

Cindy looked down at her sack full of vegetables. Was she just starving herself? Was she setting herself up to stuff like Matt did?

With that Cindy pushed back her bench, strolled over to the pizza table and snapped up the very last piece of veggie pizza. She sunk her teeth into the crunchy vegetables, gooey cheese and crispy crust. It tasted sooooooo good. She was hungry. The food was light—but not depriving. She was satisfying her hunger and her desire for food. Cindy said "no" to starving—she put away her all veggie lunch. She also said "no" to stuffing—she didn't give a second glance at the pepperoni pizza and ice cream.

Matt leaned back from the table, his stomach hurting. He didn't feel well. The starving hadn't felt good and neither had the stuffing. Maybe his SHAPEDOWN CLUB would help. This sure wasn't working.

Jesse tossed Matt a football. He caught it, almost by reflex, and tucked it under his arm. Matt grabbed his backpack and ran out the door with Jesse in hot pursuit.

SMART TALK

Losing weight doesn't mean dieting. It just means eating healthfully. It means:

Eating regular meals: breakfast, lunch and dinner

Eating mainly foods low in fat and sugar

Eating small or medium amounts

**Eating when you are hungry
and stopping before you are full.**

Let's talk about the first three, one at a time:

Eating regular meals—People who skip meals eat more than people who eat regular meals. If you skip meals you're likely to have lots of snacks. You're apt to snack on foods like chips and cookies. They have more fat and sugar than meals of turkey sandwiches do. Eating regular meals keeps your energy up all day long. A good pattern for most kids is three meals plus an afternoon snack.

Eating more foods low in fat and sugar—No foods are forbidden. All foods, including chips, french fries, candy and cookies are okay some of the time. But you will help yourself lose weight if you eat more lighter foods, foods low in fat and sugar, like an apple rather than apple pie or a baked potato instead of fries.

Eating small to medium amounts—Are cookies really going to make you fatter? No, not if you have one cookie rather than five. Nor will burgers if you have a small one rather than a double

2

cheeseburger. When you really want a sweet or fatty food, have it, but have a small amount.

How do you figure out which foods are lighter and which foods are heavier? We use the SHAPEDOWN Food Summary. It divides food into four groups: FREE FOODS and LIGHT FOODS, which you will eat more often, and HEAVY FOODS and JUNK FOODS which you will eat less often.

FREE FOODS are low in fat and sugar. They get less than 30% of their calories from fat and less than 10% of their calories from sugar. Plus they have so few calories that they don't even count. Enjoy as many FREE FOODS as you like.

LIGHT FOODS are low in fat and sugar just like FREE FOODS. They have more calories than FREE FOODS. You can eat medium amounts of them and still lose weight.

HEAVY FOODS are higher in fat and sugar. They get more than 30% of their calories from fat and less than 10% from sugar. Some are naturally higher in fat or sugar, like cheese or fruit rolls. Others have fat or sugar added in processing.

JUNK FOODS are mainly fat or sugar. They have many, many calories per bite and almost no vitamins and minerals. Some JUNK FOODS are ready to eat like potato chips. Others you add to other foods, like jam on toast. Eat JUNK FOODS only once in a while, or only in small amounts like a half teaspoon of butter on toast.

Remember, no foods are forbidden. Eat foods from all the groups. But begin to eat FREE FOODS and LIGHT FOODS more often. This week you will pick out foods you want to start eating more of and foods you want to start eating less of. Enjoy experimenting with changing foods!

In this chapter, you will write down your goals for SHAPEDOWN. They should be big enough to matter and small enough to achieve. Keep in mind these slogans:

Progress not perfection. Plan to make progress with your weight, not to solve your whole problem. Be grateful for small changes. Don't despair if you are not perfect.

Healthy bodies lose weight. Plan goals that make your body healthy. Running for an hour when you are used to a 10-minute walk is bad news for your body. So is skipping meals and skimping on breakfast. If you act healthy, you will lose weight.

Be healthy now. Don't worry about last week's cookie binge. Forget about the all-vegetable diet next Monday. Instead, focus on this moment. Act healthy right now.

YOUR TURN!

Cindy and Matt are lightening up their food. They chose the foods they want to eat more of and less of this week. Now it's your turn.

2

1. Please circle all of the FREE FOODS you like. Circle at least ten foods.

FREE FOODS	artichokes	greens	water chestnuts	plain popcorn
	asparagus	jicama	zucchini	tobasco sauce
	bamboo shoots	lettuce	water	soy sauce
	broccoli	mushrooms	mineral water	horseradish
	brussels sprouts	onions	diet soda	garlic
	cabbage	peppers	soda water	onion powder
	carrots	radishes	tea	cinnamon
	cauliflower	sauerkraut	coffee	herbs
	celery	sour pickles	broth	spices
	cucumbers	dill pickles	tomato juice	flavorings
	eggplant	sprouts	vegetable juice	mustard
	green beans	summer squash	limes	vinegar
	green onions	tomatoes	lemons	no-oil salad dressing

2. Circle all of the LIGHT FOODS you like. Circle at least ten of them.

LIGHT FOODS	non-fat milk	fish	papaya	clear soups
	low-fat milk (1%)	tuna, canned	pineapple	vegetable soups
	non-fat buttermilk	in water	peaches	bread
	reduced fat cheese	lean red meat,	plums	bagel
	low-fat cottage	all fat removed	raisins	biscuits
	cheese	apples	prunes	english muffins
	plain low-fat	applesauce, canned	strawberries	hamburger buns
	yogurt	without sugar	tangerines	low-fat crackers
	dried beans	apricots	watermelons	unsweetened cereal
	split peas	bananas	fruit, canned	hominy grits
	black-eyed peas	blackberries	in water	tortillas
	lentils	cantaloupe	fruit, canned	plain spaghetti
	refried beans	cherries	in juice	rice cakes
	turkey, light	grapefruit	potatoes	rice
	meat, no skin	grapes	sweet potatoes	bran
	chicken, light	nectarines	peas	barley
	meat, no skin	oranges	winter squash	bulgar

MATT AND THE PIZZA PARTY

2

3. Circle all of the HEAVY FOODS you eat often.

HEAVY FOODS	low-fat milk (2%)	almonds	cream soups	coconut
	whole milk	sunflower seeds	macaroni &	fries
	chocolate milk	chicken or turkey	cheese	hash browns
	cheese	with skin	macaroni salad	sweetened cereals
	creamed cottage	chicken or turkey	potato salad	granola
	cheese	dark meat	pizza	high-fat crackers
	flavored yogurt	fried chicken	chili	taco shells
	ice milk	turkey hot dogs	avocado	stuffing
	low-fat frozen	fish sticks	sauced vegetables	corn bread
	yogurt	fried fish	fruit rolls	muffins
	pudding	tuna, packed in	sweetened	pancakes
	tofu	oil	applesauce	waffles
	peanuts	red meat	fruit, canned	french toast
	peanut butter	eggs	in syrup	buttered popcorn

4. Circle all of the JUNK FOODS you eat often.

JUNK FOODS	ice cream	fruit drinks	candy	beer
	sherbet	kool-aid	chocolate	wine
	shakes	jello	chocolate topping	liquor
	cream cheese	chips	syrup	butter
	sour cream	pies	honey	margarine
	half and half	cakes	jam	oil
	whipped cream	cookies	jelly	lard
	cream sauce	doughnuts	marmalade	gravy
	bacon	pastries	sugar	mayonnaise
	sausage	croissants	popsicles	tartar sauce
	hot dogs	candy cereal	regular sodas	salad dressing
	salami	granola candy	sweet pickles	olives
	salt pork	bars	gum	salt

5. List three FREE FOODS you will eat more often.

   1. _____ 2. _____ 3. _____

6. List three LIGHT FOODS you will eat more often.

   1. _____ 2. _____ 3. _____

7. List three HEAVY FOODS you will eat less often.

   1. _____ 2. _____ 3. _____

8. List three JUNK FOODS you will eat less often.

   1. _____ 2. _____ 3. _____

9. What are your goals for SHAPEDOWN? What would you like to accomplish?

_____ I want to lose weight: 2   4   6   8   10   pounds

_____ I want to stop gaining weight.

_____ I want to get fit, move better and run faster.

_____ I want to eat regular meals—breakfast, lunch and dinner.

_____ I want to eat less food.

_____ I want to eat fewer sweet foods.

_____ I want to eat fewer fatty, greasy foods.

_____ I want to learn more about food and exercise.

_____ I want to like my body more.

_____ I want to like myself more.

2

GIVE ME STROKES

We took FAMILY TIME each day to review these records and to praise each other.

I watched no more than 0 2 4 6 8 hours of TV[1].

I EXERCISED[2] for 50 100 200 300 400 minutes or more.

I filled out correctly MY FOOD! each day.

GOAL OF THE WEEK:
I did something fun with my parent on ___ days.

	MON.	TUES.	WED.	THURS.	FRI.	SAT.	SUN.	TOTAL	MET MY GOAL?
								___ days	YES NO
								___ hours	YES NO
								___ minutes	YES NO
								___ days	YES NO
								___ days	YES NO

TOTAL NUMBER OF GOALS MET ⇒

[1] Hours per week of television:
0 = TV STAR 2 = NEWS ANCHOR 4 = GAME SHOW HOST 6 = WEATHER PERSON 8 = GAME SHOW RUNNER UP

[2] Minutes per week of exercise:
400 = STAR ATHLETE, 300 = IN SHAPE, 200 = GETTING STRONGER, 100 = GREAT START, 50 = GOOD TRY

HOW TO USE: MY FOOD!

Now you will begin writing down what you eat. It will help you pay more attention to your food. You will not be on a diet. You will still get plenty of food. You will still eat the foods you like. But you will try to eat in a healthy way.

For the next two chapters, with your parent's help you will write down everything you eat each day. Then you will check off each food as FREE, LIGHT, HEAVY OR JUNK. You will also figure out if you ate regular meals, that is, breakfast, lunch and dinner. Eating regular meals helps most people lose weight. Later you will also check to be sure you are eating many different kinds of food so that you get the vitamins and minerals you need. You will see if you are hungry when you start eating and see if you stop eating before you are full.

Here's how to use MY FOOD!: Every time you eat or drink, write down the time, the food or drink, and the amount. At the end of the day, use the FOOD SUMMARY and check the group that best fits each food:

F = FREE, L = LIGHT, H = HEAVY, and J = JUNK. Then add up each column. This will give you an idea of whether or not you are eating mainly FREE FOODS and LIGHT FOODS.

All healthy people - too fat or too skinny - should eat mainly FREE FOODS and LIGHT FOODS so that their diet is less than 30% fat. Most people find that they need to keep their HEAVY and JUNK FOODS to only a few per day to keep their diet healthy.

If you eat mainly FREE and LIGHT FOODS and begin to feel deprived, talk to your parent right away. It is very important that you do not feel deprived. If you do, you and your parent will find a way that you can have some of the foods you like a lot.

If you don't lose at least 1/2 pound in a week, you may need to exercise more, eat fewer HEAVY FOODS and JUNK FOODS or eat a little less of everything. If you want more help learning about your food, talk to your SHAPEDOWN instructor.

MY FOOD!

Day *Monday*

Time	Food or Drink	Amount	Free	Light	Heavy	Junk
6:40 am	W.W. toast	2 slices		✓		
	butter	1 t.				✓
	jam	2 t.				✓
	decaf.	2 cups	✓			
11:30 am	turkey-light	3 ounces		✓		
	french roll	1		✓		
	mustard	1 t	✓			
	diet soda	1 can	✓			
3:30 pm	apple	1		✓		
4:20 pm	lifesavers	3				✓
6:10 pm	pizza, veggie	1 slice			✓	
	salad		✓			
	frozen yogurt, non-fat	10 ounces			✓	
9:05 pm	vanilla cookies	6 small				✓

Ate mainly FREE & LIGHT Foods? yes (no)   Ate breakfast, lunch & dinner? (yes) no

25

════════ MY FOOD! ════════

Day _____

Time	Food or Drink	Amount	Food Type			
			Free	Light	Heavy	Junk

Totals
Ate mainly **FREE & LIGHT** Foods?   yes   no   Ate breakfast, lunch & dinner?   yes   no

════════ MY FOOD! ════════

Day _____

Time	Food or Drink	Amount	Food Type			
			Free	Light	Heavy	Junk

Totals
Ate mainly **FREE & LIGHT** Foods?   yes   no   Ate breakfast, lunch & dinner?   yes   no

26

Day _____

Time	Food or Drink	Amount	Food Type			
			Free	Light	Heavy	Junk

Totals
Ate mainly FREE & LIGHT Foods?   yes   no   Ate breakfast, lunch & dinner?   yes   no

2

= MY FOOD! =

Day _____

Time	Food or Drink	Amount	Food Type			
			Free	Light	Heavy	Junk

Totals
Ate mainly FREE & LIGHT Foods?   yes   no   Ate breakfast, lunch & dinner?   yes   no

Day _____

	Time	Food or Drink	Amount	Food Type			
				Free	Light	Heavy	Junk

Totals

Ate mainly FREE & LIGHT Foods?   yes   no   Ate breakfast, lunch & dinner?   yes   no

2

Day _____

	Time	Food or Drink	Amount	Food Type			
				Free	Light	Heavy	Junk

Totals

Ate mainly FREE & LIGHT Foods?   yes   no   Ate breakfast, lunch & dinner?   yes   no

Day _____

Time	Food or Drink	Amount	Food Type			
			Free	Light	Heavy	Junk

Totals

Ate mainly **FREE & LIGHT** Foods?   yes   no   Ate breakfast, lunch & dinner?   yes   no

2

Just for Fun!

FOOD FINDER'S CLUB I

The FOOD FINDER'S CLUB wants you! If you can find all of the foods listed below on the FOOD SUMMARY, you will be their next member. Remember, in SHAPEDOWN **you are not on a diet.** You are just eating healthier, something all kids - even skinny kids - should do.

Also, keep in mind that in SHAPEDOWN no foods are off limits. You can eat foods from all of the groups. Eating a healthy diet means eating most of your foods from the **FREE FOOD and LIGHT FOOD lists,** but if it is important to you to have a particular **HEAVY or JUNK FOOD,** you can have it. Just talk to your parent about it during FAMILY TIME. Together you can work out a way to have the food you want.

Are you ready to find the foods? Just look at the FOOD SUMMARY on the next page and circle the food listed below. Then write in what kind of food each one is: FREE, LIGHT, HEAVY or JUNK). READY, SET, GO!

Food   **What kind of food is it? (FREE, LIGHT, HEAVY, JUNK)**

cheese   _____

gum   _____

pizza   _____

doughnuts   _____

bread   _____

bananas   _____

flavored low-fat yogurt _____

green peppers   _____

honey   _____

turkey hot dogs   _____

Did you find all ten? Congratulations, and welcome to the FOOD FINDER'S CLUB. Later on, the inner circle of the FOOD FINDER'S CLUB will ask you to join it. More later!

FOOD SUMMARY

FREE FOODS	artichokes asparagus bamboo shoots broccoli brussels sprouts cabbage carrots cauliflower celery cucumbers eggplant green beans green onions	greens jicama lettuce mushrooms onions peppers radishes sauerkraut sour pickles dill pickles sprouts summer squash tomatoes	water chestnuts zucchini water mineral water diet soda soda water tea coffee broth tomato juice vegetable juice limes lemons	plain popcorn tabasco sauce soy sauce horseradish garlic onion powder cinnamon herbs spices flavorings mustard vinegar no-oil salad dressing

LIGHT FOODS	non-fat milk
	low-fat milk (1%)
	non-fat buttermilk
	reduced fat cheese
	low-fat cottage
	   cheese
	plain low-fat
	   yogurt
	dried beans
	split peas
	black-eyed peas
	lentils
	refried beans
	turkey, light
	   meat, no skin
	chicken, light
	   meat, no skin
		fish
		tuna, canned
		   in water
		lean red meat,
		   all fat removed
		apples
		applesauce, canned
		   without sugar
		apricots
		bananas
		blackberries
		cantaloupe
		cherries
		grapefruit
		grapes
		nectarines
		oranges
			papaya
			pineapple
			peaches
			plums
			raisins
			prunes
			strawberries
			tangerines
			watermelons
			fruit, canned
			   in water
			fruit, canned
			   in juice
			potatoes
			sweet potatoes
			peas
			winter squash
				clear soups
				vegetable soups
				bread
				bagel
				biscuits
				english muffins
				hamburger buns
				low-fat crackers
				unsweetened cereal
				hominy grits
				tortillas
				plain spaghetti
				rice cakes
				rice
				bran
				barley
				bulgar

HEAVY FOODS	low-fat milk (2%)
	whole milk
	chocolate milk
	cheese
	creamed cottage
	   cheese
	flavored yogurt
	ice milk
	low-fat frozen
	   yogurt
	pudding
	tofu
	peanuts
	peanut butter
		almonds
		sunflower seeds
		chicken or turkey
		   with skin
		chicken or turkey
		   dark meat
		fried chicken
		turkey hot dogs
		fish sticks
		fried fish
		tuna, packed in
		   oil
		red meat
		eggs
			cream soups
			macaroni &
			   cheese
			macaroni salad
			potato salad
			pizza
			chili
			avocado
			sauced vegetables
			fruit rolls
			sweetened
			   applesauce
			fruit, canned
			   in syrup
				coconut
				fries
				hash browns
				sweetened cereals
				granola
				high-fat crackers
				taco shells
				stuffing
				corn bread
				muffins
				pancakes
				waffles
				french toast
				buttered popcorn

JUNK FOODS	ice cream sherbet shakes cream cheese sour cream half and half whipped cream cream sauce bacon sausage hot dogs salami salt pork	fruit drinks kool-aid jello chips pies cakes cookies doughnuts pastries croissants candy cereal granola candy bars	candy chocolate chocolate topping syrup honey jam jelly marmalade sugar popsicles regular sodas sweet pickles gum	beer wine liquor butter margarine oil lard gravy mayonnaise tartar sauce salad dressing olives salt

2

2

Directions: After you have read chapter 2, answer this practice quiz. Check your answers below. Then complete the final quiz. At your next session, you will check the answers to the final quiz.

TRUE OR FALSE

PRACTICE

_____ 1. In SHAPEDOWN, you analyze your diet to be sure you have no more than 4 heavy foods or junk foods each day.

_____ 2. Healthy diets contain 30 percent or less fat.

_____ 3. Beef hot dogs are JUNK FOOD.

_____ 4. You must be perfect with food and exercise to lose weight.

_____ 5. A good way to lose weight is to skip breakfast.

FINAL

_____ 1. In SHAPEDOWN, you write down your food and then figure out if you ate mainly FREE FOODS and LIGHT FOODS.

_____ 2. If you ever eat a really greasy food, you'll get fat.

_____ 3. Low-fat cottage cheese is a FREE FOOD.

_____ 4. Honey is a JUNK FOOD.

_____ 5. It helps you lose weight to feel guilty about the cookies you ate yesterday.

Practice Quiz Answers: 1.F 2.T 3.T 4.F 5.F

32

3. MATT AND CINDY'S PRIVATE CLUB

Matt sat in the cozy corner of Ms. Bacon's room the day after the pizza and ice cream party with his stomach still hurting from the five pieces of pepperoni pizza and the six scoops of rocky road, strawberry and fudge vanilla ice cream.

He was writing the next sentence in his composition, "My Experience with an Unidentified Flying Object," about his plane trip to Disney World, when his pencil broke. He got up, squeezed past Cindy and strode straight to the pencil sharpener. He heard a "wapppp" and felt a sharp bump on his back. Somebody in the front row, probably David, had hit him with a spit wad.

There was a hush. Then a giggle. Matt's face turned as red as a pomegranate. They were giggling about his weight! They were laughing at him! Matt prayed that he would melt into the floor, turn into dust and blow away so that he would never have to turn around and face them all.

Matt pulled in his swollen stomach, took a deep breath, turned on his heels and walked

3

slowly back to his seat with his head held high. The class quietly went back to writing their compositions. They were quiet, that is, until Amy went up to ask Ms. Baker how to spell the capital of Nebraska, which is where she went during spring break. Then they started snickering about Amy's skinny arms.

Back in his seat, Matt lowered his head, curled his body over his desk and placed his pencil to his paper to write out the next sentence—the one that told about the flashing lights—when snap! His pencil broke again. He heard it snap, he saw the little black cone-shaped tip roll down his desk, but he didn't believe it. How could it break again?

Was life always going to be so difficult? Was he doomed to be fat because his mother was chunky and because his dad was so big? Was it written in his genes that he'd be fat forever? When would the teasing and tormenting stop?

Just then Cindy tapped him on the shoulder. He looked up to see her smiling face. She handed him a freshly sharpened pencil.

He looked over and gave her a half smile. Cindy had saved him.

Matt thought again about his family. The night before, he had watched his mother, father and sister Kate, closely. They all had eaten greasy, fatty, sugary foods. Last night his sister had eaten six chocolate chip cookies and his father seven! All they ever did was eat and watch television.

Matt's brow furrowed. Did he want a fat life or a thin life? Was eating light and exercising worth it? Yes, thought Matt, I'm not waiting around any more. I'm getting in shape right now! As he said "Now" Matt jumped in his chair. Cindy jumped, too and then they both laughed.

Cindy passed Matt a note:

"I think you're cute." All around the border of the white paper were pink hearts.

Matt read it, and wrote back:

"I'm glad we're starting SHAPEDOWN together."

Cindy blushed.

Matt wondered what would happen to his family if he started eating light, exercising and losing weight. Would they be mad at him? Would they feel that he was showing them up? Would they feel proud of him? Matt thought as he added the last sentence to his composition. "The flashing white lights were gone for now, but would they return? Perhaps, tonight!" He underlined "Perhaps, tonight!" five times and turned over his paper.

No, they wouldn't be mad at him for getting in shape. They'd be proud. Besides Matt would help them, too. Maybe Matt's weight would be a way to get his mom and dad in shape. Matt could help the whole family!

After Ms. Baker gave them their science homework assignment, Matt picked up his books and was ready to charge out the door. He stopped. Matt turned to Cindy, "Wanna ride bikes to school together tomorrow?"

Cindy nodded, "Sure, see you tomorrow at seven-thirty in front of my house," and ran out the door.

That night Cindy sat at the kitchen table and thought about Matt and bike riding. Just then Clown, now stuffed with rice crackers, hopped down from his shelf and walked across the table.

3

"Cindy," said Clown, "Have you noticed that I've filled out?"

"Yes, Clown," said Cindy affectionately, "Those rice crackers really filled you out without making you too fat."

"But Cindy," continued Clown, "Just look at my arms. Can you see any muscles?"

Cindy opened her eyes very wide and then shook her head, "Not one, Clown."

"I haven't an ounce of strength, Cindy. I can't even climb up to the top shelf to change my cookies . . . or crackers, that is. And watch this," he said bending over, "I can't even touch my knees, let alone my toes."

"Well, you're not the most flexible clown in the universe, Clown, but you're still the best cracker jar I've ever known." said Cindy standing up and bending down to touch her toes . . . and only reaching her knees.

"What's worse," said Clown, "is that I can't even walk up the hill to my cousin Owl's, who was stuffed with oatmeal raisin cookies last week. Who knows what's filling him up this week!"

"Clown, you don't have much endurance, do you? That's no fun! I'll help you, Clown. My friend, Matt and I have a SHAPEDOWN CLUB. We're getting in shape. We're starting tomorrow to do BODY STRETCHES for flexibility, BODY BUILDERS for strength and

HUFF AND PUFF exercises for endurance. We're going to get so fit that we can have fun for hours and hours without getting tired!"

"And I will be able to walk up the hill to see what kind of cookies my Cousin Owl's stuffed with, and touch my toes and climb up to the highest shelf?"

"You bet, Clown, if you exercise almost every day for an hour or more," said Cindy with a wink, and lifted Clown's hat to help herself to a cracker. "Matt and I are starting tomorrow. We're biking half an hour to school and half an hour back! That's a HUFF AND PUFF exercise."

Clown took off his hat and scratched his head. "OK, you're doing the biking to make your heart and lungs strong and to give you endurance. But what are you doing to be flexible and strong?" he questioned.

Cindy smiled, "When I get up in the morning I'm going to do BODY STRETCHES and for my BODY BUILDERS I'm going to dig in Grandpa's garden for strength.

"I wish I had a plan," said CLOWN sadly.

"You can, Clown. Just imagine ways to move your body that are fun!"

"Oh!" said Clown, "I know! For HUFF AND PUFFS, I'll walk up the hill to Cousin Owl's twice a day."

"Great. That will get your heart and lungs strong. Then you can run and play without getting tired!" replied Cindy.

Clown jumped down onto the table. "For my BODY STRETCHES, I'll touch my toes 20 times in the morning and 20 times at night. For BODY BUILDERS I'll lift all of the canned peaches, pears and plums from the bottom shelf to the top shelf and back before lunch and before dinner."

Clown leaned back and smiled. He had made his own exercise plan!

Just after dawn the next morning Cindy rolled out of bed and looked at her body in the mirror. It looked fluffy and round. She had a very comfortable body. The fat felt like it was hugging her. There were good things about letting go of extra fat, but she would probably miss the coziness of her round body.

Cindy started her morning BODY STRETCHES, stretching way up high, over to one side and then like a swing, over to the other. She imagined herself looking leaner. She pushed in her cheeks looking for her cheekbones. She felt her legs looking for muscles. If she got leaner she would still be Cindy, but just a leaner, fitter Cindy. Maybe being a leaner, fitter Cindy would be pretty cozy, after all.

The stretching felt good. With her clothes on, teeth brushed, hair combed, books in hand, Cindy ran down the stairs, spooned a bowl of wheat flakes — real cereal, not the candy-coated kind — and non-fat milk into her hungry body and raced out the door, just in time to see Matt bike up her street.

SMART TALK

Exercise is part of SHAPEDOWN because it's fun and because it makes you healthier. It also helps you lose weight, feel less hungry and changes you body from fat to lean. It gives you a "glow" and shrinks your troubles down to size. It makes you enjoy your body more.

How long do I exercise? You can quickly work up to 60 minutes per day. Start with 30. Go to 45 and then finally 60. Recess and P.E. class at school don't count. You're already doing them and still have a weight problem. That means you need more exercise.

How often do I exercise? Every day. Your body needs food every day. Your body also needs exercise every day. Otherwise the poor little blood vessels shrink, your energy-boosting enzymes go away and your body feels restless and couped up. Give your body the exercise it needs to stay pleased as punch every day.

When do I exercise? Any time is a good time, but make it a regular time - like every morning after breakfast or every night after dinner. For most kids the best time is immediately after school. That's because right then they are tired or hungry and exercise takes away that hunger and tiredness. Exercise is a great break before starting your homework.

What kind of exercise? Any kind of exercise that is safe and doesn't hurt your body when you do it is good. Standing is better than sitting. Walking is better than standing. The idea is to move.

There are three parts to fitness: **strength, flexibility and endurance.** You need all three kinds of fitness to make your body work at its best.

Strength is how strong you are - for instance, how much weight your muscles can lift. Most exercise makes you stronger. Chores like stacking firewood or carrying groceries strengthen your muscles and so do floor exercises. For instance, doing sit-ups strengthens your stomach muscles. It doesn't take the fat off your stomach, but it does strengthen the muscles underneath.

Activities that make your muscles stronger we call BODY BUILDERS.

Can you make yourself look like a pretzel? If you can, you're very, very flexible! Being flexible means you can touch your toes without a bit of strain. Activities that make your body bendable and flexible we call BODY STRETCHES. By stretching your body you teach it a lesson in acting like a pretzel.

Most kids want to run fast and be good at sports. Sure, you need to be strong and flexible for most sports, too, but mainly you need to have energy. Your body can't poop out on you half way through a game. You need to have good endurance. How do you make your heart and lungs strong so you can run and play without getting tired? With HUFF AND PUFF exercises. They are also the ones that burn up fat.

Don't go too fast. Is sprinting a good HUFF AND PUFF exercise? No! People who sprint and exercise too fast just tire themselves out and — worse — get themselves injured. Exercise in which you breathe hard (but not too hard!) like brisk walking, biking, and bouncing on the mini-trampoline burns up fat, boosts your endurance and makes your heart and lungs strong.

To be sure you are not underexercising or overexercising, take your pulse right after exercising. If for 6 seconds it is 12 to 15 beats, your exercise is just right. If it's more than 15, slow down. If it's less that 12, speed up.

How do I get ready to be lean? People have told you you should lose weight. You think that you should lose weight. But you might not be comfortable weighing less. It may feel strange. You look at your body and it doesn't look like your own. What happened to your cheeks and your stomach? They seemed to disappear.

People act differently toward you. They don't tease you as much. But also, your friends change. Maybe some of your friends will stop liking you and others will start liking you. To make yourself more comfortable with the lean body you're creating, picture yourself thinner. How does it feel? How do you look? Picture it often so that as you lose extra fat, your new lean body will seem normal.

1. Matt made up his exercise program: Stretching for 5 minutes every morning before breakfast and right before soccer for BODY STRETCHES, 30 sit-ups and 15 push-ups every night for BODY BUILDERS, and an hour of biking, soccer or the bouncer (mini-trampoline) for HUFF AND PUFF exercises. What is your plan?

BODY STRETCHES
What I will do: _____

BODY BUILDERS
What I will do: _____

HUFF AND PUFF
What I will do: _____

_____

_____

3

2. When I will exercise on week days: (Circle all that apply to you):

before school   after school   before dinner   after dinner

3. When I will exercise on weekends (Cricle all that apply to you):

morning   afternoon   evening

4. Who I will exercise with (Circle all that apply to you):

mother   father   sister   brother   friend   step-parent

neighbor   whole family   other _____

5. Cindy rested on her bed quietly. She closed her eyes and relaxed. She pictured herself becoming leaner and leaner. Her cheekbones began to show. Her face was longer and her eyes and nose looked bigger. Her arms and stomach were smaller. She felt light. It felt strange. She looked different. It felt good, mostly.

Picture yourself leaner. Describe how your face and body look different:

_____

_____

_____

6. How did it feel to be leaner? (check all that are true for you):

_____ great

_____ OK

_____ scary

_____ uncomfortable

_____ impossible

_____ bad

_____ other_____

3

GIVE ME STROKES #3

	MON.	TUES.	WED.	THURS.	FRI.	SAT.	SUN.	TOTAL	MET MY GOAL?
We took FAMILY TIME each day to review these records and to praise each other.								___ days	YES / NO
I watched no more than 0, 2, 4, 6, or 8 hours of TV[1].								___ hours	YES / NO
I EXERCISED[2] for 50, 100, 200, 300, 400 minutes or more.								___ minutes	YES / NO
I correctly filled out MY FOOD! each day.								___ days	YES / NO
GOAL OF THE WEEK: On ___ or more days, I praised my parent for something he or she did[3].								___ days	YES / NO

TOTAL NUMBER OF GOALS MET ⇒

[1] Hours per week of television:
0 = TV STAR 2 = NEWS ANCHOR 4 = GAME SHOW HOST 6 = WEATHER PERSON 8 = GAME SHOW RUNNER UP

[2] Minutes per week of exercise:
400 = STAR ATHLETE, 300 = IN SHAPE, 200 = GETTING STRONGER, 100 = GREAT START, 50 = GOOD TRY

[3] Done at some time other than FAMILY TIME.

41

3

Day _____

3

Time	Food or Drink	Amount	Food Type			
			Free	Light	Heavy	Junk

Ate mainly FREE & LIGHT Foods? yes no   Ate breakfast, lunch & dinner? yes no

Day _____

Time	Food or Drink	Amount	Food Type			
			Free	Light	Heavy	Junk

Ate mainly FREE & LIGHT Foods? yes no   Ate breakfast, lunch & dinner? yes no

Day _____

Time	Food or Drink	Amount	Food Type			
			Free	Light	Heavy	Junk

Ate mainly FREE & LIGHT Foods?   yes   no   Ate breakfast, lunch & dinner?   yes   no

---

MY FOOD!

Day _____

Time	Food or Drink	Amount	Food Type			
			Free	Light	Heavy	Junk

Ate mainly FREE & LIGHT Foods?   yes   no   Ate breakfast, lunch & dinner?   yes   no

MY FOOD!

Day _____

Time	Food or Drink	Amount	Free	Light	Heavy	Junk

Food Type

Ate mainly FREE & LIGHT Foods?   yes   no   Ate breakfast, lunch & dinner?   yes   no

MY FOOD!

Day _____

Time	Food or Drink	Amount	Free	Light	Heavy	Junk

Food Type

Ate mainly FREE & LIGHT Foods?   yes   no   Ate breakfast, lunch & dinner?   yes   no

3

44

Day _____

Time	Food or Drink	Amount	Food Type			
			Free	Light	Heavy	Junk

Ate mainly **FREE & LIGHT** Foods?   yes   no   Ate breakfast, lunch & dinner?   yes   no

3

Just for Fun!

SENSATIONAL!*

When your body moves there are lots of feelings or sensations you get. When you exercise you may feel hot, shaky, dry mouth, light or calm. It is your body and these feelings are your very own. Do these things to learn more about your feelings:

1. DO BODY STRETCHES. For 5 minutes stretch your body: up, down, around. Slowly. Don't stop.

2. STOP. LISTEN TO YOUR BODY. How does your body feel right now?

_____

_____

3. DO SIT UPS. Do sit ups for at least one minute or for as long as you can without hurting.

4. STOP. LISTEN TO YOUR BODY. Notice each feeling. How does your body feel right now?

_____

_____

6. TAKE FAST WALK FOR 30 MINUTES. Walk slowly enough so you can still talk to your parent, but quickly enough so that you breathe hard.

7. STOP. LISTEN TO YOUR BODY. How does your body feel?

_____

_____

Some feelings you may feel:

cold warm hot strong weak happy tired relaxed quiet hurt pressure clean
wet lean hard heavy light soft heart pumping blood moving shaky
nose breathing mouth dry chest heavy air inside hands tingly shoulders light

* Get your parent's and doctor's approval before doing these exercises.

3

Just for Fun!

Circle the names of vegetables in the puzzle below. Can you find all twelve? (Two are on the diagonal.)

```
S  L  E  T  T  U  C  E  O
J  S  A  P  C  C  O  R  T
I  P  K  A  A  E  L  O  P
C  I  H  R  B  L  L  M  O
A  N  L  S  B  E  A  A  T
M  A  B  L  A  R  R  I  A
A  C  S  E  G  Y  D  N  T
D  H  P  Y  E  F  I  E  O
E  T  O  M  A  T  O  S  H
```

Which of the vegetables you circled are not leaves? Please list them:

_____

_____

Name one of these vegetables that you will eat this week:

_____

Did you eat it?   YES   NO

Describe how it looked, tasted and felt:_____

_____

(Answers: horiz. - lettuce, tomato; vert. - jicama, spinach, parsley, cabbage, celery, collard, romaine and potato; diagonal - beet, pea.)

47

3

QUIZ #3

Directions: After you have read chapter 3, answer this practice quiz. Check your answers below. Then complete the final quiz. At your next session, you will check the answers to the final quiz.

3

TRUE OR FALSE

PRACTICE

____ 1. The kind of exercise that burns up fat the most is BODY BUILDERS.

____ 2. SHAPEDOWN recommends exercising every day.

____ 3. To be healthy, it is better to sprint for 10 minutes than walk for an hour.

____ 4. To figure out if you are exercising at the right pace, take your pulse after exercising.

____ 5. If you lose a lot of weight, there is a chance you may not like it.

FINAL

____ 1. HUFF AND PUFF exercises take off fat better than strength exercises.

____ 2. SHAPEDOWN recommends exercising daily for at least 60 minutes.

____ 3. Walking non-stop through a shopping mall doesn't count as exercise.

____ 4. An after-exercise pulse of 12 to 15 beats in 6 seconds is just right.

____ 5. If you lose a lot of weight, people will like you better and all your problems will disappear.

Practice Quiz Answers: 1.F 2.T 3.F 4.T 5.T

4. TRADING LUNCHES

Matt watched Cindy run out of her house, grab her bike and pedal down her driveway toward him. Cindy looked pretty and vibrant today. She carried her books under her arm . . . but where was her lunch? For that matter, where was Matt's lunch?

"Lunch," said Matt. "Lunch."

"Oh, I forgot!" exclaimed Cindy.

"We both forgot."

"Let's just buy it at school, Matt," suggested Cindy, "it's so easy."

"Cindy, people in our SHAPEDOWN CLUB think that greasy stuff at school is gross!"

"Oh!" said Cindy, throwing her head back and rolling her eyes. "They're right. It is gross. You can just see the grease and fat oozing out of the fries and dripping off the burritos. Yuck!"

"And crusted sugar flaking off the doughnuts. Sticky sugar in candy ready to breed bugs on your teeth. Gross!" added Matt.

49

"We could go to the market down the street, the one with the video games," suggested Cindy.

"The only choices they have are sodas, candy and all that fat food you pop into the microwave. There isn't a real piece of food in the place!" cracked Matt.

"I know!" said Cindy, "Let's go to my house and fix our own lunches."

With that, the two members of the SHAPE-DOWN CLUB ran through the back screen door and into the kitchen. They could hear Cindy's mother and grandfather upstairs getting ready for the day.

Matt opened the refrigerator and saw a big yellow bowl of veggies, crisp, fresh and ready-to-eat. "There's our lunch right there," said Matt with a noble nod.

"Matt, lunch shouldn't just be veggies. People lose extra fat all the time by eating regular food, not just celery sticks. Straight veggies will just make you feel hungry and deprived and then you'll just, you'll just . . . . "

"I know. Binge. Right?" said Matt looking rather sheepish.

"Yes, you're right. Food is something to eat when you're hungry. It's not something to feel guilty about or afraid of. Let's make a lunch that's light but that will take away our hunger and taste good!

"I know how to load up on hamburgers, fries, sodas, chips and cookies, and I know how to starve myself. I guess I haven't learned yet how to eat!"

"Simple. Just eat lots of different kinds of

LIGHT FOODS and FREE FOODS. Let's make a lunch for each other and trade. We'll both be surprised at lunch time!"

Matt and Cindy raced around the kitchen, peeking in the cupboard, refrigerator, and even inside Clown. They each chopped, stirred, spread, sliced and bagged a lunch. Suddenly, they heard Grandpa's steps on the stairs. In a wink, Matt and Cindy, bag lunches in hand, quietly slipped out the back screen door, ran for their bikes and were off to school.

The wind whistled by their ears, leaves danced around their wheels and the morning air froze their noses and reddened their cheeks. Up the hills they huffed and puffed. Down the slopes they soared, and finally landed at school. Giggling and shouting they tossed the lunches to each other. Each then held a surprise bag.

By lunch time Matt just knew he'd guessed everything in the lunch, just from feeling the bag. Cindy's bag felt like it had a round hard lump in it and a few soft, squishy things. The lunch bell rang and they were off to the lunch area. But Amy stopped them, "Want a cherry fruit roll? I've got an extra!"

Cindy looked at Matt. She didn't want Amy to know she was trying to lose weight. Matt quickly whispered in her ear, "Just say, 'No thanks.'"

Cindy said, "No thanks, Amy." Amy looked quizical. Everybody loves fruit rolls. Oh well, thought Amy, I'll just ask someone else.

"But Matt," protested Cindy, "shouldn't I give her a reason? What will she think?"

"You could say, 'No thanks, I'm not hungry.' or 'No, thanks, I have enough lunch.' But all you

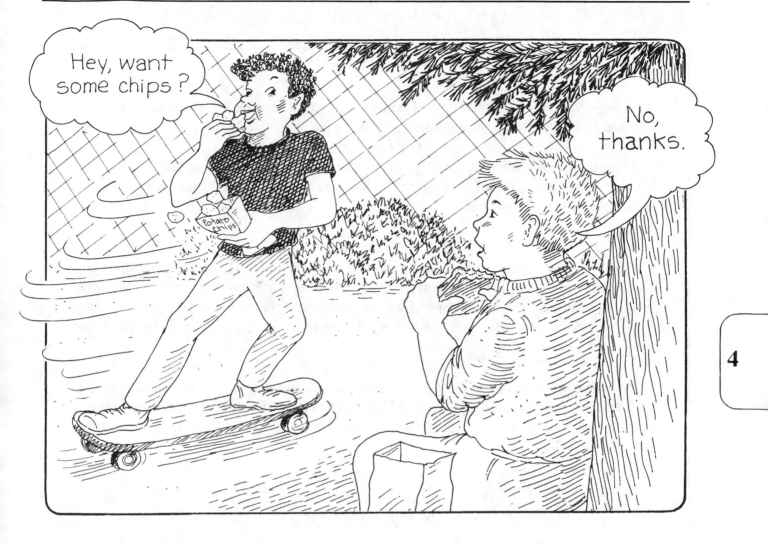

really need to do is say 'No thanks.' What she thinks is not as important as what you think. You need to take care of yourself, not to worry about what everyone thinks. Besides, if she stops being your friend because you didn't eat her fruit roll, she wasn't much of a friend anyway."

Cindy listened and knew Matt was right. She liked their club. They were really helping each other.

Cindy and Matt found a place to eat on a bench under a large pine tree and hurriedly tore open their bags.

Matt discovered a turkey sandwich on whole wheat with—not mayonnaise—but ketchup. A big, sweet orange sliced up and a small carton

of non-fat milk. He was hungry and bit right into his sandwich.

Just then David sailed by on his skateboard—which is not allowed in the lunch area. "Hey, Matt, want some chips?" he said, stuffing a handful into his mouth.

"No thanks," said Matt.

Cindy tore open her bag. In it was her old red thermos filled with vegetable soup, a baggie of carrot sticks and another baggie of celery. And two crackers from Clown's tummy. Cindy laughed. Three servings of veggies and one of grains. That's progress, Matt!" and she laughed as she munched on a sweet, crisp carrot stick.

─SMART TALK─

Eating—Your parents will tell you when it's time to eat and the foods you can have. You will decide whether you eat and how much you eat.

It is your parent's job to be in charge of the times and kinds of food you eat. You control whether or not you eat and how much you eat. That is your job. Nothing goes into your mouth that you don't put there.

How do you decide how much to eat? If the food is a HEAVY FOOD or a JUNK FOOD you eat very little of it. If it's a FREE FOOD or a LIGHT FOOD you eat more of it. You also decide based on your hunger. If you've been eating way more than your body needs, your body can fool you. You have trained your body to want more food. If you start exercising and eating less, soon your body will get back to normal. Then it will give you some idea of how much food you need.

Eat a little more when you feel hungry and a little less when you don't feel as hungry. Eat until you are just satisfied, not stuffed. Look at the HUNGER SCALE below. When you feel the hunger vanish, stop right then. Push away your plate when you are just satisfied. You are done.

... very hungry

... hungry

just ... satisfied

full ...

very full ...

Fixing lunch — Lots of kids fix their lunches on school days, for picnics or for weekend lunches. What's a healthy bag lunch? A basic healthy lunch is:

a whole or half sandwich

a piece or two of fruit

a baggie full of veggies

non-fat milk

water

Pack as many veggies as you like. Use whole wheat or other whole grain bread because it gives you a whole wallop more nutrition than white bread does.

Pay attention to whether you have fatty foods in your sandwich. Bread is a LIGHT FOOD, but most of the things you put between bread are heavy. Steer clear of more than a smidgen of mayonnaise, and stick to turkey and other low fat meats rather than greasy fillings like salami and oil-packed tuna. Why? Because fat goes to fat. Fat has more than twice the calories of carbohydrates and proteins.

Speaking up — Sometimes people will offer you food when your parents aren't around. Kids at school will offer you chips and granola bars. Grandmothers and neighbors will push cookies on you. You can take these foods every time your parent isn't looking. But that won't make you feel good. You'll feel like you did something you weren't proud of. You'll weigh yourself each week and find that you haven't lost weight.

Remember that eating is a private and personal choice. It is your choice. Only you put food in your mouth. Nobody else puts it there but you. When you're on your own — at a friend's or at school — you will make choices for yourself. Don't eat just because someone offers you food. You are not a little child. You are almost a teenager and you are more responsible than a little child is. You can make choices you are proud of.

When someone offers you food, think about three things:

1. Is it time to eat (breakfast, lunch, snack or dinner)?

If it isn't, don't eat.

┌───┐
─── **SMART TALK continued** ───

2. Is the food a LIGHT FOOD or FREE FOOD?

If it isn't, **don't eat it.** Eat your meal or snack later. Or **do eat it** but eat only half of it.

3. Am I hungry?

If you aren't hungry, eat little or none of it. Wait until your next meal or snack to eat.

When you decide not to eat something someone offers you, tell them directly. Just say "No thanks!," "No, thanks I'm not hungry." or "No thanks, I don't feel like cookies right now." Speak up politely and directly and say, "No, thanks!"
└───┘

4

YOUR TURN!

1. Matt practiced listening to his hunger signals. He practiced eating when he was hungry and stopping eating when he was just satisfied. He tried to stop before he was full or very full. Circle how you felt before and after three meals of your choice. From now on, practice listening to your hunger signals whenever you start or stop eating.

Day	Meal	How I felt when I started eating:	How I felt when I stopped eating:
_____	breakfast lunch dinner	very hungry hungry just satisfied full very full	very hungry hungry just satisfied full very full
_____	breakfast lunch dinner	very hungry hungry just satisfied full very full	very hungry hungry just satisfied full very full
_____	breakfast lunch dinner	very hungry hungry just satisfied full very full	very hungry hungry just satisfied full very full

2. Look at your FOOD SUMMARY at the back of this book. Find the FREE FOODS and LIGHT FOODS you enjoy. Fill up your lunch bags below with two lunches that are light and taste good.

4

3. Look at the FOOD SUMMARY again. List three LIGHT FOODS you would like to have for afternoon snacks this week:

_____

_____

_____

4. Now pick three FREE FOODS vegetables you would like to have for afternoon snacks this week:

_____

_____

_____

5. Think about the three questions to ask yourself when someone offers you food. Remember the three questions:

1. Is it time to eat (breakfast, lunch, snack or dinner)?

2. Is the food a LIGHT FOOD or FREE FOOD?

3. Am I hungry?

Describe one time this week when you asked yourself these three questions.

_____

_____

_____

4

6. If you decided that you did not want the food someone offered you, what would you say?

To a friend who offers you a cookie:

_____

To your mother or father who offers you a bag of chips (even parents sometimes offer you food that isn't good for you):

_____

To a grandmother or older friend who wants to buy you a candy bar:

_____

GIVE ME STROKES #4

	MON.	TUES.	WED.	THURS.	FRI.	SAT.	SUN.	TOTAL	MET MY GOAL?
We took FAMILY TIME each day to review these records and to praise each other.								___ days	YES NO
I watched no more than 0 2 4 6 8 hours of TV[1].								___ hours	YES NO
I EXERCISED[2] for 100 200 300 400 minutes or more.								___ minutes	YES NO
I correctly filled out MY FOOD! on 4 or more days.								___ days	YES NO
GOAL OF THE WEEK: We went on a family walk on ___ or more days.								___ days	YES NO

TOTAL NUMBER OF GOALS MET ⇒

[1] Hours per week of television:
0 = TV STAR 2 = NEWS ANCHOR 4 = GAME SHOW HOST 6 = WEATHER PERSON 8 = GAME SHOW RUNNER UP

[2] Minutes per week of exercise:
400 = STAR ATHLETE, 300 = IN SHAPE, 200 = GETTING STRONGER, 100 = GREAT START,

57

4

USING THE FOOD GUIDE PYRAMID WITH MY FOOD!

Use the **Food Guide Pyramid** to help you eat better every day. It will help you make sure you eat different kinds of foods and get enough vitamins, minerals and protein. Each of these groups provides some, but not all, of the nutrients you need. No one group is more important than another — for good health you need to eat some foods from each of the groups. Go easy on fats, oils, and sweets, the foods in the small tip of the Pyramid.

It is recommended that you eat **at least 3** servings from the **Milk** group, **2** from the **Meat** group, **3** from the **Vegetable** group, **2** from the **Fruit** group, and **6** from the **Grain** group. You probably will need more food than that or you will lose more than one pound a week. Try to get most of this food from fruits, vegetables, breads and cereals. They give you vitamins and minerals and are low in fat.

Important! You are not on a diet. You should not be trying to eat a strict pattern of **3Milk-2Meat-3Vegetable-2Fruit-6Grain.** If you do, you are dieting and dieting doesn't work. Instead, use the **3-2-3-2-6** numbers to get an idea of how healthy you are eating. Are there groups in which you don't consume any foods? Do you eat mainly fruits and grains or meat and milk? Get a feel for whether or not your eating is healthy. Try to do well, but don't worry about being perfect.

Look at the **Food Guide Pyramid** below to get a feel for the amounts you should eat from each food group:

The Food Guide Pyramid
A Guide to Daily Food Choices

Fats, Oils, & Sweets
USE SPARINGLY

Milk, Yogurt, & Cheese Group
3 SERVINGS

Meat, Poultry, Fish, Dry Beans, Eggs, & Nuts Group
2-3 SERVINGS

Vegetable Group
3-5 SERVINGS

Fruit Group
2-4 SERVINGS

Bread, Cereal, Rice, & Pasta Group 6-11 SERVINGS

KEY   ● Fat (naturally occurring and added)

▼ Sugars (added)

These symbols show fat and added sugars in foods.

Developed as a cooperative effort by: The United States Department of Agriculture and The United States Department of Health & Human Services

4

What counts as "one serving" depends on the type of food. If you have a tall, 12 ounce glass of milk you have 1½ servings. One piece of fruit counts as 1 serving. Just ¼-cup of nuts is a serving but 2 full cups of lettuce is also 1 serving. The table below gives some examples of serving sizes for various food groups.

This week record what you eat on the MY FOOD! form for only four days. At the end of each day, in addition to checking off the type of food, also check off the Food Group (Milk, Meat, Vegetable, Fruit, Grain). Then add up the checks for each group to see how you compare to the recommended 3-2-3-2-6 Pyramid Guide.

PYRAMID FOOD GROUPS

GROUP	SERVINGS	FOODS	SERVING SIZE
Milk	3 children 2 adults	milk yogurt cottage cheese cheese frozen yogurt	1 cup 1 cup 1½ cups 1½ ounces 2 cups
Meat	2	beans, lentils meat, fish or poultry nuts eggs peanut butter	1 cup 3 ounces ¼ cup 2 4 tablespoons
Vegetable	3	lettuce potato vegetables	2 cups 1 ½ cup
Fruit	2	fruit juice canned fruit	1 piece 6 ounces ½ cup
Grain	6	bread or tortilla cooked cereal, rice or pasta hamburger bun cold cereal small roll or muffin	1 piece ½ cup ½ 1 ounce 1

Try to eat a citrus fruit/juice & a dark green leafy vegetable or yellow fruit/vegetable daily.

4

== MY FOOD! ==

Day _____

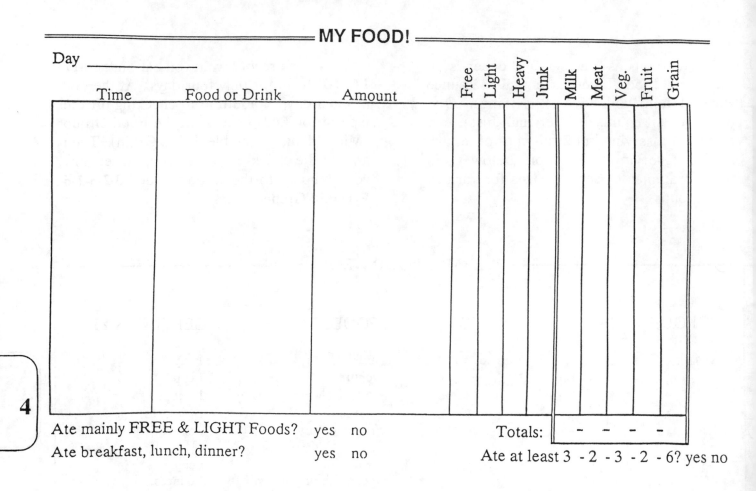

Time	Food or Drink	Amount	Free	Light	Heavy	Junk	Milk	Meat	Veg.	Fruit	Grain

Ate mainly **FREE & LIGHT** Foods? yes no

Ate breakfast, lunch, dinner? yes no

Totals: – – – –

Ate at least 3 - 2 - 3 - 2 - 6? yes no

4

== MY FOOD! ==

Day _____

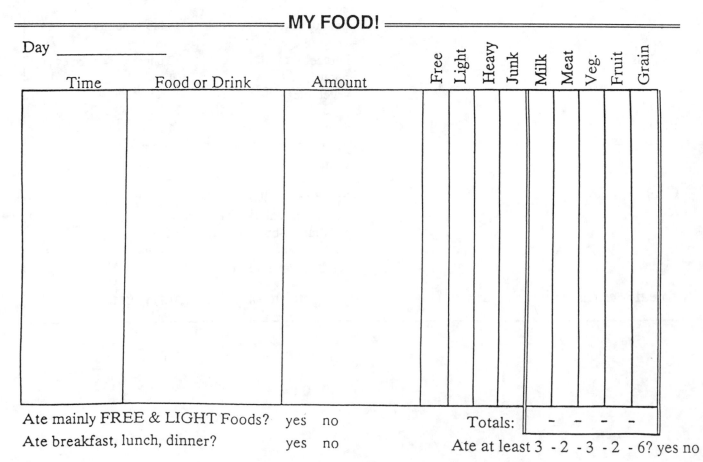

Time	Food or Drink	Amount	Free	Light	Heavy	Junk	Milk	Meat	Veg.	Fruit	Grain

Ate mainly **FREE & LIGHT** Foods? yes no

Ate breakfast, lunch, dinner? yes no

Totals: – – – –

Ate at least 3 - 2 - 3 - 2 - 6? yes no

═══ MY FOOD! ═══

Day _____

Time	Food or Drink	Amount	Free	Light	Heavy	Junk	Milk	Meat	Veg.	Fruit	Grain

Ate mainly FREE & LIGHT Foods?   yes   no

Ate breakfast, lunch, dinner?   yes   no

Totals: -   -   -   -

Ate at least 3 - 2 - 3 - 2 - 6? yes no

═══ MY FOOD! ═══

Day _____

Time	Food or Drink	Amount	Free	Light	Heavy	Junk	Milk	Meat	Veg.	Fruit	Grain

Ate mainly FREE & LIGHT Foods?   yes   no

Ate breakfast, lunch, dinner?   yes   no

Totals: -   -   -   -

Ate at least 3 - 2 - 3 - 2 - 6? yes no

Directions: After you have read chapter 4, answer this practice quiz. Check your answers below. Then complete the final quiz. At your next session, you will check the answers to the final quiz.

TRUE OR FALSE

PRACTICE

4

____ 1. If a friend offers you a cookie, you have to take it.

____ 2. It is healthy to have a snack when you are not hungry.

____ 3. A baked potato topped with a teaspoon of sour cream is a LIGHT FOOD.

____ 4. Peanuts, bananas and grapes are all LIGHT FOOD snacks.

____ 5. When a friend's mother offers you cookies, it's OK to say "no, thanks".

FINAL

____ 1. To a parent who suggests you go out for ribs, you can say, "No thanks, I don't want to eat heavy stuff."

____ 2. If you are hungry in the afternoon, it's healthy to have a piece of fruit.

____ 3. A fried taco is a LIGHT FOOD.

____ 4. Bread, bread sticks and bananas are all LIGHT FOOD snacks.

____ 5. If you go to a party, you must eat all the food you are served.

Practice Quiz Answers: 1.F 2.F 3.T 4.F 5.T

5. MATT'S MAGIC WORDS

Matt sat in Ms. Bacon's class the next morning with his shoulders hunched forward, his head hung low and his face filled with a frown. He looked like he had lost his best friend, like his bike had just been run over by a truck and like nobody remembered his birthday. Matt looked glum.

He reached into his pocket when Ms. Bacon wasn't looking, searching until he found the chocolate covered peanut butter candy. He curled his fingers around the candy and waited. Ms. Bacon turned to the blackboard to explain a division problem. Matt's hand darted from his pocket to his mouth. His teeth crunched the brittle chocolate coating and his tongue relished the creamy peanut butter filling. He began to feel a shade, a tad, a bit less glum.

Cindy, Amy and Jesse watched as Matt's hand slid slowly into his pocket again. They watched his glum face relax as he popped another piece of chocolate covered peanut butter candy into his down-turned mouth. They could hear him crunch on the brittle chocolate coating and could imagine the creamy peanut butter swirling around his mouth.

5

Just then Clown appeared on Matt's shoulder. Cindy jumped, "Clown, they'll see you. Ms. Bacon will, I know it!"

But Clown just smiled his easy smile and winked at her. And then in his most gentle voice replied, "But Cindy, my dear, your friend, Matt, is sad and is using food to try to cure his sadness."

"Clown," said Cindy, "The whole world cures sadness with food. Why should Matt be any different?"

"But my dear Cindy," replied Clown, "Food doesn't cure sadness, madness, boredom, anxiety or even loneliness. Food cures hunger. Why do you think he has to eat five handfuls of chocolate covered peanut butter candy? Because food is not very good at making bad feelings go away."

Cindy thought for a moment, "You mean, choose a solution that fits the problem?"

With that Clown jumped from Matt's shoulder, did a double somersault onto Matt's desk, "Whoopee, you got it, Cindy!"

Cindy scratched her head, twirled her hair around her index finger and continued, "So you cure sadness by crying, madness by punching a pillow, boredom by getting busy, anxiety by relaxing in a hot bath, and loneliness by calling a friend?"

Clown smiled affectionately at Cindy, "You can also cure difficult feelings by opening up and talking about them. When you talk about how you feel, it doesn't seem so bad. And you can discover ways to fix the feelings, too."

Clown was so thrilled and proud of his wisdom that his nose started to glow. Matt, Amy and Cindy caught a glimpse of the glow. No one else besides the kids in the cozy corner of Ms. Baker's room could see Clown.

"Okay, Clown, I heard what you said. Are you making fun of me?" said Matt threateningly.

Clown quivered with fear. "Oh no, Matt. I'd never make fun of anybody bigger than a cookie jar!"

Matt's face softened, "I don't know how to open up, Clown. I do know how to spell Mississippi, read Dicken's stories and solve some algebra problems. But opening up—I just don't know the ABC's of it. When I feel bad, I usually just eat."

Clown looked at the four kids in the cozy corner, "Does anybody here know the magic words of how to open up?"

Cindy twirled her hair. Amy thought with the tip of her tongue at the corner of her mouth. There was a crease down the middle of Jesse's forehead that touched his glasses.

Ms. Bacon put up another set of math problems on the board. They thought some more . . . the magic words of how to open up . . . what could they be?

"I know," said Amy, jumping up. "The magic words are 'I feel . . .' and then you put after that whatever you feel!"

"So, instead of eating five handfuls of chocolate covered peanut butter candy, I could write a note to Cindy that said, "I feel sad."

"Exactly," agreed Clown, "and you could tell her what you were sad about."

5

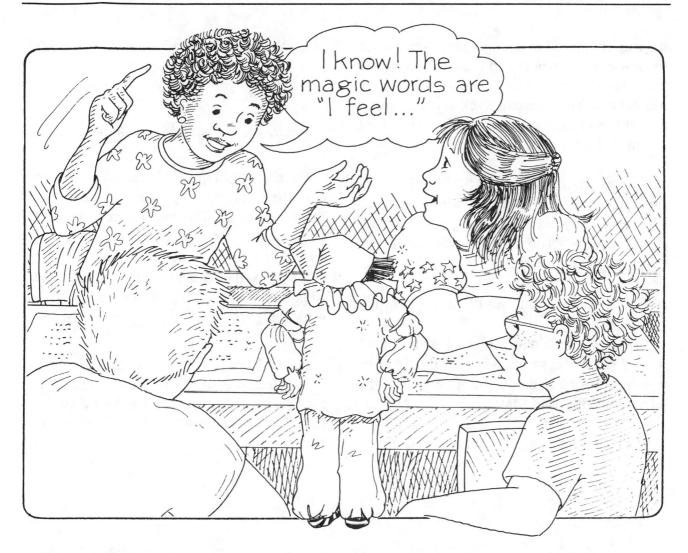

"That's difficult," replied Matt, "Lots of times I'm not sure what I'm sad about. In fact, I'm not absolutely sure it's sadness. I'm feeling a little mad, too."

"Terrific, Matt," beamed Clown, "You don't need to know what you're feeling or why before you open up. As you talk about it you learn more about your feelings and you try to figure out why you're feeling that way."

"You mean," said Amy, "You just start with the magic words, 'I feel .' and see what comes out?"

"That's exactly right, my sweet face," said Clown.

Matt looked up at the ceiling, down at the floor, "I feeeeeeeel . . . ." He looked through the windows to the birch trees past the fence, "I feel sad and angry and confused . . . "

"That's right, that's exactly right, Matt" said Clown. "Those are your feelings. You have a right to those feelings. Nobody can say you are wrong to feel that way. If you feel it, you feel it. That's it. Now . . . what are you feeling sad, angry and confused about?"

"I don't know," said Matt staunchly. "I just don't know."

"Try harder, Matt. What do you think you feel sad, angry and confused about?" said Amy. "Guess!"

"I feel sad, angry and confused because I'm

making changes. I'm eating lighter — except for today — exercising more and I've lost 3 pounds of fat. That's 12 cubes of butter, you know. But my mother and father are still stuck to the television and still pouring on the chips, salami and ice cream. It isn't fair."

"I know, Matt," said Cindy, "Talk to them. Tell them how you feel. Tell them what you want. They can always turn you down, but there's no chance that they'll do what you want unless you tell them what you want."

"What do you want, Matt?" asked Clown.

"I want to go on family hikes. I want my dad to play catch and soccer with me. I'd like to be not the only one using the trampoline while the television's on," said Matt.

Clown smiled his wide smile, "You did it,

Matt. You opened up and talked about your feelings. You used the magic words, 'I feel . . .' and decided what you want. You are a star!"

"Yeah, you're a star, Matt!" shouted Cindy.

The room went quiet. Ms. Bacon's eyes turned red with anger, "Cindy, Matt, Amy and Jesse, I feel that your attention has drifted. It has drifted so far away that I'm not convinced that you understand these division problems. In fact, the only way I will be convinced is if you each do ten additional sets of math problems for your homework tonight."

So as Clown faded very slowly until only his broad smile remained, the kids in Ms. Bacon's cozy corner thought about the magic words, "I feel . . ." and the ten sets of math problems that were due the next day.

5

SMART TALK

Managing difficult feelings--You feel down. You're upset. You go to the cookie jar but know that you really aren't hungry. Eating those cookies won't make you feel up; they won't make you feel better.

Almost any difficult feeling can trigger some kids to eat. They have learned to eat when they feel sad, mad, bored, worried or lonely. When they feel especially bad inside they can eat a whole bag of cookies.

Eating to stuff away difficult feelings doesn't work. Think of difficult feelings as big, locked doors. On the other side of the doors are happy, peaceful feelings. To open the door you must find the right key.

The only key that opens the door of loneliness and gets rid of all those difficult feelings is the key of people. Being with people you like opens the door of loneliness and brings you into the meadow of happy, peaceful feelings.

The only key that opens the door of boredom is the key of activities. Doing something you enjoy shoos away boredom and opens the door to happy, peaceful feelings.

Food only opens the door of hunger. When you use the key of food on your doors of sadness, anger, boredom, anxiety or loneliness, it doesn't work. While you're eating you don't think about your difficult feelings. But as soon as you stop eating, the difficult feelings come back. The door slams shut and you are closed off once again from happy, peaceful feelings.

SMART TALK continued

When you feel badly stop everything. You are important. The fact that you aren't feeling well matters. Think about how you are feeling. Figure out what you need to make yourself feel better. Find the "key" that fits your lock. Here are some examples of healthy ways to make difficult feelings better:

Open up and talk about your problem — Keeping it inside just makes things worse. Talk with your friend, parent, neighbor, teacher, dog, cat or anyone you trust. Talking about it helps you figure out what the problem is and gives you ideas for solving it.

Tell people how you feel — You have a right to how you feel. Nobody can tell you that your feelings are wrong. Talk about your feelings. Getting your feelings out is a big relief. Just start your sentences with the magic words "I feel . . . " and keep talking.

If people don't listen to you, tell them — Lots of times parents don't know how to listen very well. If you don't feel like they are listening to you, tell them. Politely say, "I don't feel listened to."

Write it out — What if there is no one to talk to? Get a notebook and make your own journal. Write down your fears, worries and secrets. It helps!

Move your body — Exercise lifts your spirits and makes the sad and mad monsters go away. Get some exercise to make your outlook happier.

Relax for a few minutes — Take some time just for yourself. Lie down on your bed. Breathe deeply and let your mind feel calm and relaxed.

Say good things to yourself — Be sure that the voice inside is friendly and encouraging. All day long you talk to yourself. Be sure that this "self-talk" is positive and loving. Say to yourself, "I'll be fine," "It will work out," or "It's okay not to be perfect." Be your own best friend.

Matt was feeling awful. How did he know that he felt awful? He noticed that after school he was starving. All he could think about was food. So he lay down on his bed and relaxed. He needed time to think. "I am feeling . . . . . worried." Good, that was a first step. But he didn't know what he was worried about. Matt called his mother at work. "Mom, I'm feeling worried but I don't know what I'm worried about." They talked for a while and Matt realized that he was worried about school. He hadn't been getting his homework done on time. Matt and his Mom figured out a way that he could get more time for homework.

Matt found that the door blocking good feelings was worry and that the key to unlock-

SMART TALK continued

ing that door was more time for homework. The only way he figured it out was by starting with the magic words, "I feel . . .

Cindy found herself thinking about sweets all the time. She usually thought about food when she had difficult feelings. Cindy walked out the front door and around the back garden where Grandpa was weeding around the tulips and the daffodils. "Grandpa," said Cindy, "I feel awful."

"So do I," Grandpa replied, "it's my back that bothers me, especially when I garden. Now pick up that hoe and get busy."

"Grandpa," said Cindy loudly, "I don't feel listened to. I have some bad feelings and I want to talk about them."

Grandpa looked up from his weeding, "Okay, Cindy, I'm listening."

Cindy started, "I feel . . . I don't know what I feel . . . I feel sad about Mom and Dad's divorce. It's been a while, but I still feel sad about it. And besides, Mom has no time to spend with me any more." Cindy continued talking until she realized that she should talk to her Mom about it directly.

That night at bedtime Cindy told her mother that she was still sad about the divorce and that she needed to spend more time with her. Her mom started crying and said that she missed time with Cindy, too. They agreed to take Sunday afternoons off to do something fun together.

Cindy found that the door blocking happy, peaceful feelings was sadness. The key opening that door was spending more time with her mother. Besides, she felt better just having talked to Grandpa and Mom about it rather than keeping it all bottled up inside.

5

Sometimes you feel many different feelings at the same time. Matt feels confused, angry and sad when he gets a bad grade on a test he studied hard for. Cindy feels frustrated and unimportant when her Grandpa doesn't listen to her.

Sometimes feelings pile up. The more layers of feelings that pile up the worse it feels. When you feel really angry, sometimes it doesn't stop. The anger just sits inside of you and fumes. It feels stuck in your chest like it won't ever get out.

Think of the things you are angry about - like not getting enough time with one parent or kids teasing you at school or getting bad grades. That anger is a pile-up of feelings. There are lots of feelings buried under the anger. You need to dig them up, one at a time and set them free. If you feel each of these feelings, one at a time, they will disappear. Guess what's far below the anger? Love. Love is a warm, wonderful feeling.

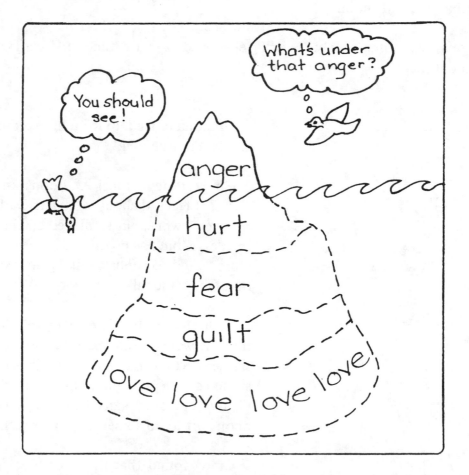

Here's how it worked for Matt: He felt angry, furious and mad that he got a "D" on his report on education in early Rome. He had worked all Sunday afternoon on it. Ms. Bacon passed back the papers. He spotted the grade, shoved the paper into his desk and slammed the desk top. Cindy jumped. Matt fumed. How could Ms. Bacon do this to him? The bell rang. In the school yard, Matt stomped back and forth between the two cherry trees. "Feel your feelings", he said to himself. Anger. He felt it in his chest like a hot red ball. Ms. Bacon was a terrible teacher. She didn't know how to grade a paper. He hated her for giving him the "D". Matt stopped. The anger had slipped away.

He dug down. How did he feel? Hurt. It hurt to get the "D". He was a good student. He tried hard. It felt awful to get that grade. The hurt drifted away.

What did he feel? Fear. Was he stupid? He was afraid he just wasn't smart enough. He'd get bad grades and get in trouble with his mom. The fear passed.

What was that now? Guilt. Guilt that he hadn't worked all that hard on Sunday. He had the television on the whole time. He really could have done a better job.

As the guilt drifted away, he noticed warm feelings, love. Maybe the paper wasn't the best he could do. Ms. Bacon was just trying to help him. He liked Ms. Bacon and he liked himself, too.

You can have warm, fuzzy loving feelings more by cleaning up your pile of feelings. You can clean up your feelings pile-up by writing a LOVE LETTER. It's a letter you write to yourself or to other people very close to you - like your parents. You write a few sentences about each of your feelings: starting with anger, then hurt, fear, guilt and, finally, love. It makes the bad feelings melt away and leaves you with feelings of love. You can learn how to write one. Your SHAPEDOWN teacher and your parents can teach you if you need some help.

A guide to writing your own LOVE LETTER is on the next page:

5

A LOVE LETTER

Dear **_Sam_**

1. Anger (I don't like it when you . . . I hate it when you . . . I am tired of . . . .)

I'm tired of helping out when you are sick and not getting any thanks from you. I think I should be appreciated. I'm mad at you.

2. Sadness (I feel sad when . . . I feel hurt because. . . I feel awful . . .)

I feel hurt because you take me for granted.

3. Fear (I feel afraid . . . I'm scared that . . . I fear that . . .)

I'm afraid that I will help you too much and have no fun myself.

4. Guilt (I'm sorry that . . . I didn't mean to . . . I feel guilty for . . .)

I feel guilty for not wanting to help you more. I'm sorry that you are sick.

5. Love (I love you because . . . Thank you for . . . I understand that . . .)

I understand that you are sick and can't help it. I'm glad you're my brother.

Love, **_Kathy_**

P.S. I need you to: *say "thank you."*

YOUR TURN!

1. Matt and Cindy have decided to learn more about their feelings. They want to stop eating to stuff away difficult feelings. By figuring out their feelings they will be able to find the "key" that fits the lock and open the door to happy, peaceful feelings. Which of these feelings have you had in the last week? (check all that are true for you):

_____ sad   _____ angry

_____ mad   _____ worried

_____ lonely   _____ tired

_____ embarrassed   _____ hungry

_____ happy   _____ depressed

_____ bored   _____ anxious

_____ hurt   _____ confused

2. Name one of the feelings you have often:

_____

3. What do you do when you feel this way? (check all that are true for you):

_____ keep it to myself/don't say anything   _____ hit somebody or something

_____ talk to a friend   _____ hurt myself

_____ talk to my mother   _____ watch television

_____ talk to my father   _____ listen to music

_____ talk to my brother of sister   _____ do homework

_____ talk to another close friend/relative   _____ get busy doing something

_____ write down my feelings   _____ eat some food

_____ exercise   _____ cry

_____ relax by myself for a few minutes   _____ fight with my brother, sister or friend

_____ say good things to myself   _____ other_____

5

4. What do you plan to do next time you feel this way?

_____

5. Most people feel difficult feelings every day. The next two times you feel badly, pause and figure out exactly how you are feeling. Write the feeling on the door below. Then figure out what you need to feel better. Write that on the key below. For instance, if Matt felt bored, he would write "bored" on the door below. If what he needed was an activity to interest him, he would write "activity" on the key. Now it's your turn!

6. Name two people you will start talking to more often about how you feel:

_____

7. A healthy diet includes lots of different foods from the Pyramid Food Groups. Write at least three foods you like in each group below. Choose them mainly from the FREE FOODS and LIGHT FOODS.

Milk group 1. _____

2. _____

3. _____

Meat Group 1. _____

2. _____

3. _____

Vegetable Group 1. _____

2. _____

3. _____

Fruit Group 1. _____

2. _____

3. _____

Grain Group 1. _____

2. _____

3. _____

4. _____

5

GIVE ME STROKES #5

We took FAMILY TIME each day to review these records and to praise each other.

I watched no more than 0 2 4 6 8 hours of TV[1]

I EXERCISED[2] for 100 200 300 400 minutes or more.

I correctly filled out MY FOOD! on 4 or more days.

GOAL OF THE WEEK:
I played a sport with my parent on ____ or more days.

[1] Hours per week of television:
0 = TV STAR 2 = NEWS ANCHOR 4 = GAME SHOW HOST 6 = WEATHER PERSON 8 = GAME SHOW RUNNER UP

[2] Minutes per week of exercise:
400 = STAR ATHLETE, 300 = IN SHAPE, 200 = GETTING STRONGER, 100 = GREAT START,

	MON.	TUES.	WED.	THURS.	FRI.	SAT.	SUN.	TOTAL.	MET MY GOAL?
								____ days	YES NO
								____ hours	YES NO
								____ minutes	YES NO
								____ days	YES NO
								____ days	YES NO

TOTAL NUMBER OF GOALS MET ⇒

76

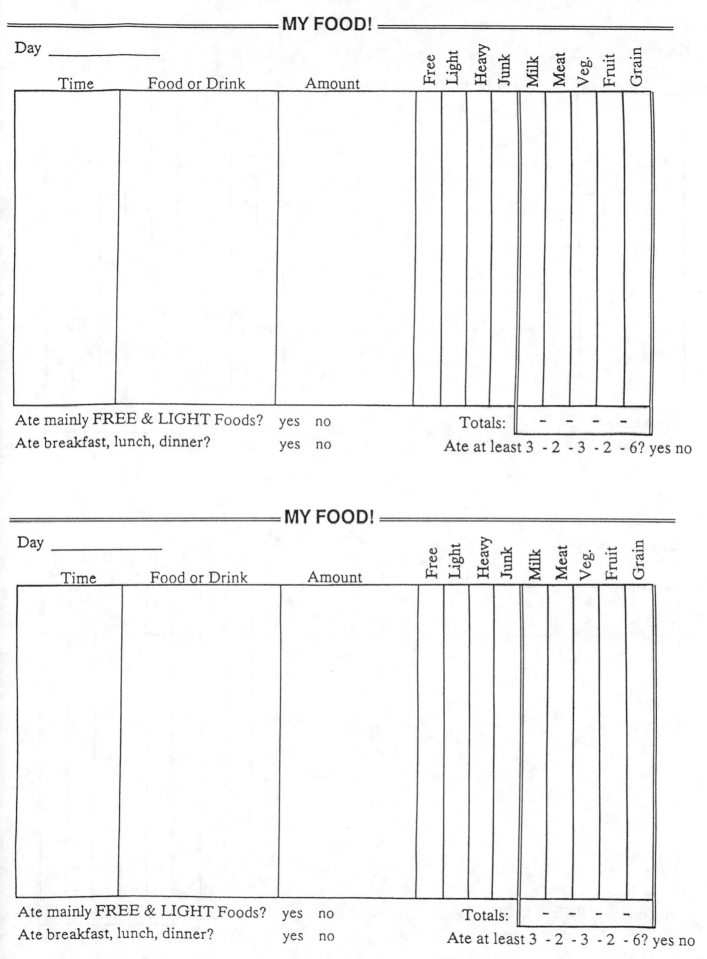

═══════ MY FOOD! ═══════

Day _____

Time	Food or Drink	Amount	Free	Light	Heavy	Junk	Milk	Meat	Veg.	Fruit	Grain

Ate mainly FREE & LIGHT Foods?　yes　no

Ate breakfast, lunch, dinner?　yes　no

Totals:　—　—　—　—

Ate at least 3 - 2 - 3 - 2 - 6? yes no

5

═══════ MY FOOD! ═══════

Day _____

Time	Food or Drink	Amount	Free	Light	Heavy	Junk	Milk	Meat	Veg.	Fruit	Grain

Ate mainly FREE & LIGHT Foods?　yes　no

Ate breakfast, lunch, dinner?　yes　no

Totals:　—　—　—　—

Ate at least 3 - 2 - 3 - 2 - 6? yes no

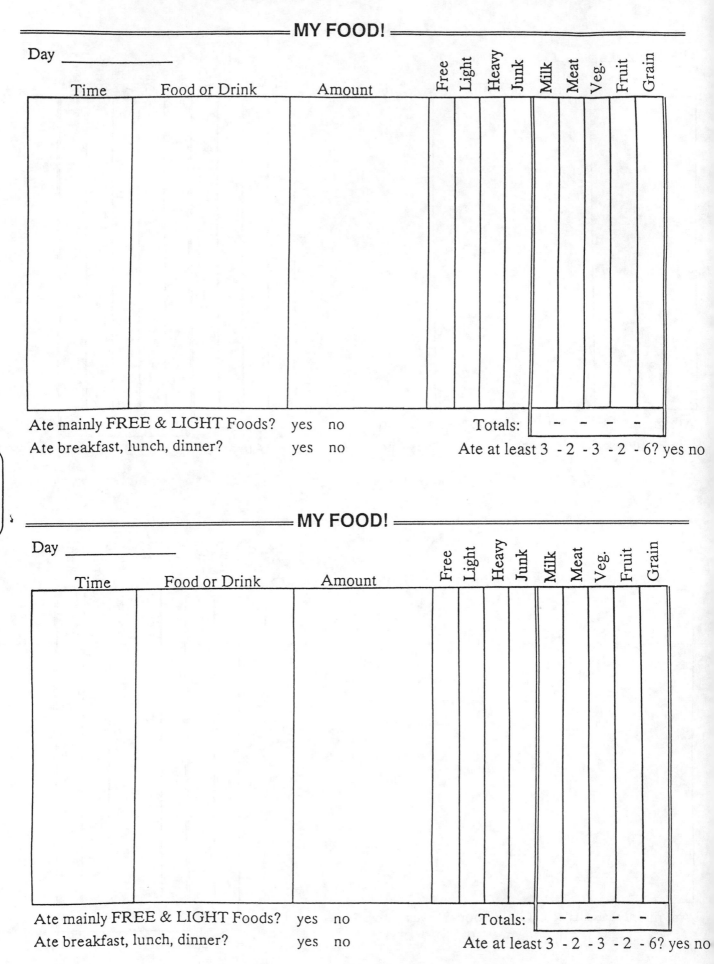

═══════════════════ **MY FOOD!** ═══════════════════

Day _____

Time	Food or Drink	Amount	Free	Light	Heavy	Junk	Milk	Meat	Veg.	Fruit	Grain

Ate mainly FREE & LIGHT Foods? yes no

Ate breakfast, lunch, dinner? yes no

Totals: – – – –

Ate at least 3 - 2 - 3 - 2 - 6? yes no

5

═══════════════════ **MY FOOD!** ═══════════════════

Day _____

Time	Food or Drink	Amount	Free	Light	Heavy	Junk	Milk	Meat	Veg.	Fruit	Grain

Ate mainly FREE & LIGHT Foods? yes no

Ate breakfast, lunch, dinner? yes no

Totals: – – – –

Ate at least 3 - 2 - 3 - 2 - 6? yes no

THROW A POTATO PARTY

Potatoes are LIGHT FOODS. They have vitamins and minerals and no fat. Enjoy them! Have a potato party. Find low fat toppings you like.

Look for toppings in the grocery store and at home.

Check out the cupboard. Look for herbs and spices that you like. Find sauces that don't have fat in them. At the grocery store find new herb mixtures, spices, seasonings and sauces to try. Here are some toppings that have been kid-tested and rate three star reviews!

lemon juice	sliced green onion	barbeque sauce
taco sauce	garlic powder and dill	plain yogurt
spaghetti sauce	fat free butter (powder or liquid)	lemon pepper
cinnamon sugar	cottage cheese	ketchup

Bake some potatoes.

Pick out some plump potatoes—one per person. Wash them well. Slit the skin with a sharp knife. Pop them into the microwave or into the oven and cook them until they are soft and fluffy. Cut them into bite-sized pieces—the skin and all. Divide them up, putting them on small plates. Use a different topping on the potatoes bites on each plate.

Enjoy your potato tasting!

Bite into each piece and taste it. How did it taste? Rate them each below.

Topping I tried   How I liked it

                              bad   OK   good

_____   1   2   3   4   5

_____   1   2   3   4   5

_____   1   2   3   4   5

5

Directions: After you have read chapter 5, answer this practice quiz. Check your answers below. Then complete the final quiz. At your next session, you will check the answers to the final quiz.

TRUE OR FALSE

PRACTICE

__ 1. It is wrong to feel sad.

__ 2. When you feel angry, you shouldn't let anybody know.

__ 3. If children listen carefully to their feelings, they can figure out what they need to feel better.

__ 4. Eggs are in the MILK GROUP.

__ 5. Potatoes are in the VEGETABLE group.

FINAL

5

__ 1. It is OK to feel sometimes that you hate your sister.

__ 2. Parents should make their children feel comfortable telling them the absolute and complete truth.

__ 3. Blocking out bad feelings with eating doesn't make the feelings go away.

__ 4. Refried beans are in the VEGETABLE group.

__ 5. Peanut butter is in the MEAT group.

Practice Quiz Answers: 1.F 2.F 3.T 4.F 5.T

6. SKATE BOARD MANIA

At recess Cindy and Amy were walking on the pathway to the office. Just as they came around the corner David crashed into them — and bowled them over. The girls fell to the pavement and David crashed to the ground. His skateboard kept careening down the path until it hit a prickly bush, rolled end over end, only stopping when it smashed into the plum tree that shaded the office.

Cindy's ankle burned! Little shavings of skin — like tissue paper — covered the wound on her ankle. Behind the white shavings bright red blood threatened to pour through the skin. "A bad scrape," thought Cindy. She looked over at Amy crying and rubbing her right knee.

Amy yelled at David, "Look what you did! Look what happened to my knee!" A drop of blood rolled down her shin from the deep gash below her knee cap.

David hung his head, found his skateboard and went on skating, this time a little more slowly. Amy turned to Cindy, "I feel so angry! He didn't even apologize! He didn't care that he hurt us! I can't believe how rude he was. And just think, he's going to get away with it! I feel so frustrated and powerless! He bloodies my body and gets off scot-free!"

Cindy nodded her head and said nothing.

Amy continued, "No, he's not going to get off scot-free. I'm going to tell Sophia at the office. She'll know what to do." Amy stomped off to the office.

Cindy stood next to the bushes. She didn't know how she felt. She didn't know what to say. The only thing she felt for sure was hungry. Maybe she didn't feel exactly starving but she definitely wanted something to eat. Food would help.

Wait. Cindy thought of the magic words, "I feel. . ." How she felt mattered. She sat down on the bench and thought, "How do I feel?"

Just then Clown popped onto her shoulder and did a front flip onto the pavement, "That's a good question, Cindy, how do you feel?"

"Not good."

"That's a start. How else do you feel?" said Clown.

"I feel bad about being quiet. I should have said what Amy said. I was mad. I did feel hurt. I wanted David to at least say he was sorry," said Cindy looking down at the pavement. A bluejay hopped along the pavement looking for bread crusts, found one and then flew away. Her eyes followed the bird as it flew up to the plum tree where he landed and quickly gulped down his bounty.

Clown thought. At times like this he wished he were only a silent cookie jar. He knew Cindy felt badly, but didn't know just what to say to her. Finally, Clown leaned forward, "Why didn't you say something, Cindy?"

"Because . . . " she said, watching the bluejay hop onto the lunch table, pick up a stray apple core and fly up over the office roof and out of sight.

"Because, why?" probed Clown, still feeling somewhat timid.

"Because, if I did say what was on my mind, David would have teased me. He has the biggest mouth at school. He loves to laugh at me and call me fat-so or tub-o."

Cindy burst into tears — big tears, the kind that jump out of your eyes and run to the ground and make big wet drops on the pavement. She held her head in her hands and wept some more.

Now Clown really wished he were just a cookie jar. He didn't care what kind of cookie jar. A soldier would be fine. Even a pig cookie jar would do, just so that he wouldn't have to see Cindy looking so sad.

Cindy looked up at Clown's mournful face, "Clown, what are you feeling?"

"I'm feeling sad . . . and helpless. I want to help you feel better but I don't know how," answered Clown.

Cindy smiled and brushed away the last tear.

Clown shook his head and a smile suddenly appeared on his face just like a light bulb turning on, "I know! Listen to me right now, Cindy. We have some serious talking to do."

"We do?" asked Cindy.

"We certainly do," replied Clown. "David was rude, but you were passive. You hung back and

6

didn't say what you thought. You didn't tell any-body how they could help you, either. You need to spit it out and tell people your thoughts, feel-ings and needs — to speak up rather than to clam up."

"I know, and I'm doing better at it than I used to. But David is right when he says I'm fat and ugly. It hurts me so much when he says it," replied Cindy, with another tear threatening to fall from her eye.

"Oh," said Clown, "I get it. All that matters is whether you're fat or skinny. If the scale goes up you're ugly, and if it goes down you're not. How you look is based on weight and that's it."

"Maybe." replied Cindy.

"And your appearance," continued Clown, is all that matters. You are how you look. Nobody cares whether you're kind, funny, loving, honest, courageous, hard-working, or talented."

Cindy got up.

Clown went on, "So let's just line up all the kids in your class one after another. We'll weigh each one and then we'll line them up in order of their weight. The ones that weigh the least will get awards for being great people and the ones that weigh the most will be given awful people awards."

Cindy laughed, "You're right. It's dumb. Even if he calls me fat-so it hurts but it doesn't hurt that much. He's just acting rude. He's really a pest. Everybody knows it. If he keeps acting pesty he'll have no friends left at all."

Clown was relieved. He let out a huge sigh.

"And you're right on another thing, Clown," said Cindy, "I like my body. Sure, I'm losing some of my extra fat, but even if I were fat forever it doesn't mean I'm ugly. It just means I have more fat than other people do. I still have pretty blue eyes, a nice smile, pink cheeks, strong legs, and smooth skin."

Clown nodded. "You're right, Cindy, even if I stay a little bit scrawny my whole life my body will still be very lovable. See this nose? How could I ever wish or hope for a better nose than this? Even Cousin Owl's nose is not straighter or more perfectly shaped," he said lifting his nose in the air and touching it gingerly.

"Clown, you sound like all that matters is how you look. Is that all you are, a ceramic pot of a cookie jar?" demanded Cindy.

"Why no, Cindy, I have lots of good qualities," said Clown hesitantly.

"Sure you do. You know when to talk and when to be quiet. You care about people — and other cookie jars — and you do great flips!" observed Cindy with a slow smile forming on her lips.

"Thanks, Cindy," said Clown and his white skin turned to a rose colored blush. Clown stood up very straight, coughed three times and said, "Okay, Cindy, it's your turn. It's easy to see the good qualities in other people. It's harder to see them in yourself. Name three of your good qualities."

"Oh, that's easy," replied Cindy confidently. She paused. She scratched her head. She looked around for that bluejay. He must have headed off to another playground.

"I'm listening . . " prompted Clown.

"Let's see, " said Cindy, "I'm funny."

"That's one."

"I'm . . . honest," Cindy continued.

"Just one more."

"I'm good at talking about my feelings!" Cindy said proudly.

"Yes, you are, my not-so-round-fluffy-or-soft friend," laughed Clown. The bell rang. "Now what are you going to do?"

"I'm going to wash off this scrape and go to class," replied Cindy.

"What about David?" asked Clown as he began to slowly disappear.

"If I'm feeling mad I'll tell him so. I'm going to say what I think and tell him I want an apology. If he teases me about weight, I'll ignore him. I'd rather be round than rude and pesty. Besides, everybody gets teased about something. I wonder what kids will tease me about after I get the rest of this extra fat off? Oh, well, Clown . . . Clown, where did you go?"

Cindy could think of another thing good about Clown. He was smart. He was helping her love herself and her body and to speak up about her thoughts, feelings and needs. She'd have to remember to give him a hug for that!

6

SMART TALK

Speaking up — You've already learned how to speak up and say, "no thanks" to food. You've also started opening up and talking about your feelings. The magic words "I feel..." let you know what's going on inside you. That is very important because you need to know how you truly feel in order to figure out what you need. If you know what you need, you can ask for it.

You are as important as any other person on earth. You have a right to your feelings. You are entitled to have needs. You don't have to take care of all your needs by yourself. You have a right to ask the people close to you for help. People who don't feel their feelings, know their needs and request help from others are usually lonely and sad. But you can use the magic words and make your life go well. You won't need to bury your lonely, sad feelings in food or in television. You'll be too busy enjoying your life.

Your parents and the other people who love you want to know how you feel and what you need. They need and want to know how they can help you. But all that love and all that help can never get to you unless you use the magic words because nobody can read your mind. What you need and feel change day to day, minute to minute. Only you can have your fingers on your own heart beat. Only you know what you feel and need.

What do you do? Just start your sentences with the magic words:

> **I feel . . .**
>
> **I need . . .**
>
> **Would you please . . .**

Is speaking up rude? No. You are just stating your thoughts, feelings, needs and problems. That's not rude. You start your sentences with the word "I." This is important. Use "I" sentences. Watch the difference. Which sentence is rude?

I need a new tennis racquet.

You have to get me a tennis racquet.

That's right, the "I" sentence is not rude. The "you" sentence is. Your thoughts, feelings, needs are important. You have a right to have them and by using "I" sentences you can tell others your thoughts, feelings and needs without being rude.

6

Handling put-downs — Nobody likes people teasing them. It hurts. You probably don't like it when people tease you about weight. You feel ashamed and embarrassed. You feel differently. What can you do about put-downs? Think about the idea that it happens to almost everybody. Everybody is different in some way — taller, shorter, fatter, thinner. In fact, once you get the extra fat off your body there will probably be some person at school who will tease you about something else.

Think about the poor person who is saying those things. He or she is rude and pesty and doesn't have many friends. That person also probably feels ashamed of being so hurtful and rude. Aren't you glad that you are not hurtful, rude and pesty?

What can you do about kids teasing? Put them in their place. Once they don't feel so powerful, it won't be fun to them to tease you. The best bet is to take a power stance. Stand tall and proud. Act proud of yourself and your body. Pesty teasers shy away from kids that don't look like victims.

Talk back to them in a way that turns the tables and makes them look foolish. Examples: "You noticed I'm fat. Very good! Now what is this, a nose, right? You are really catching on! Keep on practicing!" or "What did you say? Huh? I can't hear you. What did you say?" Be proud and they will back off. Later, talk to your mom, dad or someone else close to you. Tell them how you feel. Talk it out, then let it go. If your brother or sister teases you, talk to your mom or dad. You should not have to put up with put-downs from your family.

Liking your body — Some people think that the only thing that's important is how they look. If they don't look "perfect" they hate themselves. If they aren't at a "perfect" weight, they think they are a failure. They are afraid to get on the scale because they will feel like a bad person if they weigh too much. What a sad way to live, never accepting and loving your body — imperfections and all.

A happier, healthier attitude is that your weight is only one part of how you look. And how you look is only one part of you. Bodies come in many sizes and shapes. Whatever its size and shape, your body is likable and lovable. You probably have some favorite parts of your body. Everybody does. And you probably have some parts you don't like as well. Everybody else does, too.

Take five minutes of ME TIME each day to think about the things that you like about your wonderful body. That way you can develop good feelings about your body Keep in mind the things you like about yourself that have nothing to do with how you look. Think about how kind you are, how smart you are, how truthful you are, how well you shoot baskets or remember your lines for a play. Be "up" about yourself!

6

YOUR TURN!

1. Cindy is going to speak up more often. She will talk to her mom and grandpa about her problems. Check off all the problems you have now. If some of my problems aren't listed, add them to the bottom of the list.

_____ getting out of bed on time

_____ getting to school on time

_____ remembering to bring home my jacket

_____ remembering to bring home my homework

_____ doing my homework on time

_____ not doing well in school

_____ not having anyone to play with

_____ having an argument with a friend

_____ other kids teasing me

_____ remembering to exercise after school

_____ not eating too much with friends

_____ arguing with my brother or sister

_____ feeling sad about mom and dad arguing

_____ feeling worried about money

_____ eating too much after school

_____ feeling worried about someone who is sick

_____ feeling upset about someone who died

_____ feeling lonely

_____ feeling bored

_____ feeling angry

_____ feeling sad

_____ feeling like I don't get enough attention from mom

_____ feeling like I don't get enough attention from dad

_____ feeling sad about not seeing one of my parents enough

_____ feeling afraid of someone hurting me

_____ feeling ashamed or worried about a secret

_____ other problems:_____

_____

6

When you speak up, you talk to someone about your troubles. You tell them what you think, feel, and need. Pick two of the problems you checked above and talk to someone about them.

Remember to use the magic words: "I feel . . ." "I need . . ." " Would you please . . ."

One of my problems: _____

    To whom I will talk: _____

    What I will tell them: _____

    _____

    Did I speak up?   yes   no   unsure _____

    The magic words I used: "I feel . . ." "I need . . ." " Would you please . . ."

Another of my problems: _____

    To whom I will talk: _____

    What I will tell them: _____

    _____

    Did I speak up?   yes   no   unsure _____

    The magic words I used: "I feel . . ." "I need . . ." " Would you please . . ."

2. Who teases you about your weight?

_____

Check what you will do about these put-downs:

    ___ Think that everybody gets teased about something.

    ___ Think that the person is rude and a pest, has few friends and is probably ashamed for being so hurtful.

    ___ Take a power stance. Stand tall and proud.

    ___ Speak up and make them look foolish.

    ___ Talk to someone close about how it feels to be teased.

    ___ Something else: _____

6

3. Name five things about how you look that you like:

1._____

2._____

3._____

4._____

5._____

4. Name three things you have done that you are proud of:

1._____

2._____

3._____

5. Name three of your good qualities — things you like about yourself like your sense of humor, your kindness to people, your honesty, your generosity, your voice, your strength, your gracefulness, and so on.

1._____

2._____

3._____

6

6. Take ME TIME. Stop. Right now. Think of three things you like about yourself. Which things did you think of?

1._____

2._____

3._____

7. How did you feel after taking ME TIME?

better   the same   worse

GIVE ME STROKES #6

We took **FAMILY TIME** each day to review these records and to praise each other.

I watched no more than 0 2 4 6 8 hours of TV[1].

I EXERCISED[2] for 100 200 300 400 minutes or more.

I correctly filled out MY FOOD! on 4 or more days.

I said the **Magic Words**[3] to my parent on ____ or more days.

GOAL OF THE WEEK:

	MON.	TUES.	WED.	THURS.	FRI.	SAT.	SUN.	TOTAL	MET MY GOAL?
								____ days	YES NO
								____ hours	YES NO
								____ minutes	YES NO
								____ days	YES NO
								____ days	YES NO

TOTAL NUMBER OF GOALS MET ⇒ [ ]

[1] Hours per week of television:
0 = TV STAR 2 = NEWS ANCHOR 4 = GAME SHOW HOST 6 = WEATHER PERSON 8 = GAME SHOW RUNNER UP

[2] Minutes per week of exercise:
400 = STAR ATHLETE, 300 = IN SHAPE, 200 = GETTING STRONGER, 100 = GREAT START,

[3] "I feel . . .", "I need . . .", or "Would you please . . ."

6

90

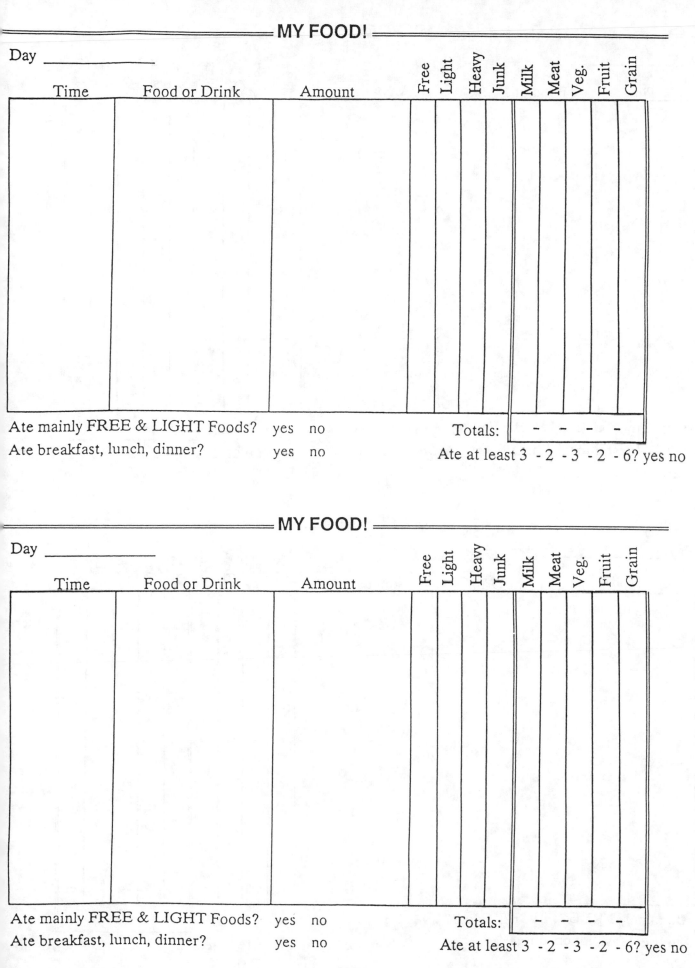

MY FOOD!

Day _____

Time	Food or Drink	Amount	Free	Light	Heavy	Junk	Milk	Meat	Veg.	Fruit	Grain

Ate mainly **FREE & LIGHT** Foods?   yes   no

Ate breakfast, lunch, dinner?   yes   no

Totals: –   –   –   –

Ate at least 3 - 2 - 3 - 2 - 6? yes no

MY FOOD!

Day _____

Time	Food or Drink	Amount	Free	Light	Heavy	Junk	Milk	Meat	Veg.	Fruit	Grain

Ate mainly **FREE & LIGHT** Foods?   yes   no

Ate breakfast, lunch, dinner?   yes   no

Totals: –   –   –   –

Ate at least 3 - 2 - 3 - 2 - 6? yes no

6

91

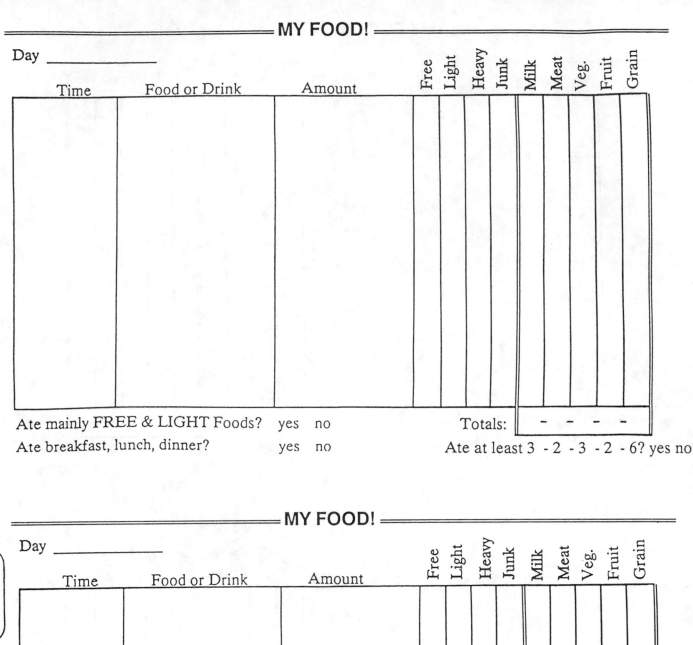

MY FOOD!

Day _____

Time	Food or Drink	Amount	Free	Light	Heavy	Junk	Milk	Meat	Veg.	Fruit	Grain

Ate mainly **FREE & LIGHT** Foods?   yes   no

Ate breakfast, lunch, dinner?   yes   no

Totals: –   –   –   –

Ate at least 3 - 2 - 3 - 2 - 6? yes no

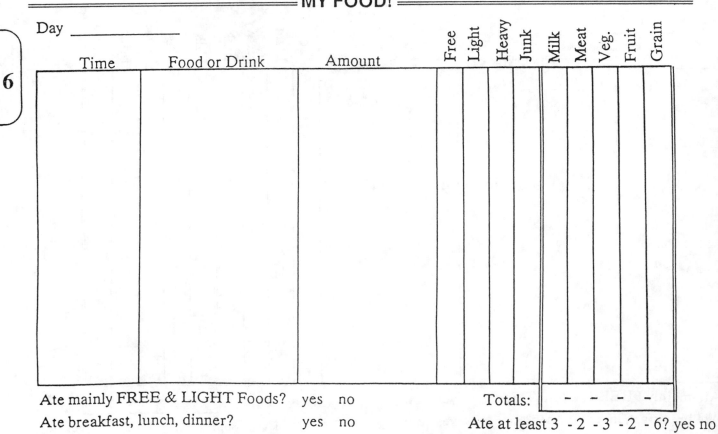

MY FOOD!

6

Day _____

Time	Food or Drink	Amount	Free	Light	Heavy	Junk	Milk	Meat	Veg.	Fruit	Grain

Ate mainly **FREE & LIGHT** Foods?   yes   no

Ate breakfast, lunch, dinner?   yes   no

Totals: –   –   –   –

Ate at least 3 - 2 - 3 - 2 - 6? yes no

Just for Fun!

FUN WITH FRUITS

Circle the kinds of fruit in the puzzle below. Can your find all 12 of them? (4 are on the diagonal)

```
A  G  U  A  V  A  D  C
C  P  A  P  A  Y  A  I
A  O  P  E  A  R  T  V
S  M  R  L  I  M  E  M
A  D  E  A  E  P  S  A
B  S  G  L  N  N  O  N
A  I  C  H  O  G  E  G
F  S  P  R  U  N  E  O
```

Name one kind of fruit you will try this week. Try it and then describe it.

Fruit I will eat this week: _____

How this fruit looked, smelled and tasted: _____

My three favorite kinds of fruit: 1. _____

2. _____

3. _____

Directions: After you have read chapter 6, answer this practice quiz. Check your answers below. Then complete the final quiz. At your next session, you will check the answers to the final quiz.

TRUE OR FALSE

PRACTICE

___ 1. People should be able to guess how you feel.

___ 2. If a parent doesn't spend enough time with a child, a child should use the **Magic Words** to tell him or her.

___ 3. Only overweight children get teased at school.

___ 4. All that matters about a person's appearance is how much he or she weighs.

___ 5. Healthy bodies come in many sizes and shapes.

FINAL

___ 1. If you want people to know exactly how you feel, you need to tell them.

___ 2. Pretending you don't feel badly, makes the feelings go away for good.

___ 3. People who tease other people usually don't like themselves.

___ 4. A person who is very overweight can still be a truly great person.

___ 5. In order to be healthy, you have to be very thin.

6

Practice Quiz Answers: 1.F 2.T 3.F 4.F 5.T

7. MATT'S CRAVINGS

Matt sat in the cozy corner reading about the Boston Tea Party. He wanted a tea party, too. Or make it a pizza party. Or an ice cream bash. Yes, that would do. An ice cream bash with six flavors of ice cream, hot fudge, marshmallow sauce and butterscotch topping, maybe some nuts and cherries and definitely gobs of whipped cream. After two months of turkey on whole wheat bread, apples and bananas he was ready for a diet revolt.

Matt wrote a note to Cindy and slipped it across to her when Ms. Baker left the room to take Nathan, who had just thrown up, to the office to call his parents. Cindy opened the note slowly. It said, "Dear SHAPEDOWN buddy, I know I'm getting in shape and I really like it but I feel like a food revolt right now. I want to go on the rampage and eat everything in sight. Your friend, Matt."

Cindy sighed. Uh oh. Here Matt goes again, thought Cindy. Another pizza and ice cream binge was in the making. For the last two months Matt had looked so happy. He had brought LIGHT FOODS to school for lunch. He had played football a lot and had been running faster. He even had been making some touchdowns.

7

95

The other boys always wanted to play with him now. Matt had to do something to keep himself from blowing it.

Cindy wrote back, "You're just having a craving. It will pass. Think about how great it feels to make those touchdowns," and she passed her note to Matt just as Ms. Bacon entered the room.

Matt slid the note into the middle of his opened history book. When Ms. Bacon went back to grading papers he carefully snuck the note from his book and unfolded and read it. Cindy didn't understand, thought Matt. He **really** craved ice cream. It had been building in him for a whole month. Yesterday he had even snuck a candy bar from his father's top drawer. Now he wanted more.

"Snuck a candy bar, huh?" said a voice. Clown appeared, perched on Matt's pencil rack.

"Yes," replied Matt, looking down at the pencil he was twirling.

"What made you decide to have a candy bar?" asked Clown.

"I felt deprived. I haven't had candy in two months," said Matt "and I was feeling bored and lonely after school."

"Food doesn't solve boredom, getting busy does. It doesn't solve sadness, or anger either. The thing that it solves well is hunger. Just like water solves thirst. Did sneaking the candy bar make you feel better?" asked Clown.

"Yes. I mean no. I liked the sweet chocolate taste, but that only lasted about 90 seconds. Then I felt worse. I was mad at myself. And disappointed. Sneaking feels like lying. It feels bad," replied Matt.

"If you decide to eat a candy bar, just eat it. Don't feel guilty. Don't sneak," said Clown.

"But if my parents knew I ate a candy bar they'd be red hot mad," replied Matt.

"Untrue. False. Wrong. Your parents love you. They care more about you than about how fat you are. If you're feeling deprived they will help you work out a way to eat a candy bar. But they can't help you unless you tell them how you are feeling," said Clown crossing his legs.

"You really mean it?" said Matt. Clown nodded. "That makes me relax inside. I can really talk with them about what I'm thinking and feeling! It's funny. I've stopped craving ice cream now that I know I can always work out a way to have it."

The bell rang. Clown disappeared instantly. Cindy approached Matt, "Let's talk, Matt."

"That's okay, Cindy. My cravings vanished. When I want something I can work out a way to get it."

"How?" asked Cindy.

"Trade-offs," replied Matt.

"Trade-offs?" questioned Cindy.

"Yes, like every once in a while when I crave an ice cream cone, I can eat only half a sandwich for lunch, then have my cone. That's a trade-off. I work them out with my parents during FAM-ILY TIME. Easy, huh?"

"Yeah, easy," replied Cindy wondering what miracle had struck Matt.

"Can you come over after school tomorrow? We can go on a bike ride or play some tennis and then have dinner," said Cindy.

7

"Sounds great!" said Matt.

The next day after school Cindy and Matt rode on their bikes to Cindy's house. They hit tennis balls against the garage door, listened to music and then helped out with dinner. They set the table and made a salad, washing the lettuce, slicing the ripe, red tomatoes and the crisp cucumbers.

Finally, dinner was ready. They had a huge green salad with a little dressing sprinkled on top, a big baked potato with a tiny dab of butter and sliced turkey breast with cranberry sauce. Yummmmm.

Cindy's mom and grandpa, her half-brother Michael and Matt savored the hot turkey and crunched on the crisp salad. Cindy and her family talked about their days. What went well and what didn't and how they were feeling. It was peaceful and fun. Michael had followed a football into the bushes, right into a yellow jacket's nest and had been stung on the nose. Cindy's grandfather had won $5 in the lottery. Cindy had done better at math and had made a new friend at school named Nicola. Cindy's mom talked about the new secretary at work. She was from New York City and knew all about the new Broadway plays there. Matt was quiet.

Finally, he blurted out, "This is not dinner. This is too calm and peaceful. There's no television blaring, no people ignoring each other, no gulping down food. This is strange!"

There was a hush. Then mom spoke, "This is

7

how we like to eat. We're in the habit of enjoying our food and each other. On days when someone is grouchy or too tired, they talk about it. We try our best to make meals relaxing, a time we can be together."

"Oh," said Matt, "In my house we go and come as we please. The television's usually on. Sometimes we eat dinner. Other times we just snack all night."

"There's nothing wrong with that, Matt," said Michael. "If it works well for your family and doesn't make you eat too much, it's just fine."

"But when we snack instead of have dinner, I eat three bowls of cereal and half a box of crackers. And when I watch television and eat I don't even taste my food. I don't think it works that well."

So as Mom, Grandpa, Michael, Cindy and Matt had seconds on salad, Matt thought about convincing his family to change their eating style. They cleared the dishes and Matt said his goodbye's and thank you's and rode home with the full moon lighting up the countryside. Matt felt at peace. It had been a very good day.

7

SMART TALK

Cravings—Have you had cravings yet? Cravings are when your mouth wants something so badly that your brain can think of nothing else. If you have a chocolate craving you walk around with a chocolate bar glued to your brain. You keep thinking about that chocolate bar. You want chocolate and you want it right now! That's a craving.

What do you do about cravings? You find out what's causing them. What causes cravings? Several things. Habit is one cause. You're used to eating the food and now you miss it. Deprivation is another cause. You've been over-doing your healthy eating so you feel deprived. Another cause is hunger. If you're skipping meals or not eating enough at meals you may get so hungry that you crave foods. Still another is feelings. If you're feeling depressed, lonely or angry, you may crave sweets or breads. So the main reasons for cravings are habit, deprivation, hunger and feelings.

The solution to cravings is to tell your parent during FAMILY TIME that you are having a craving. Your parent will help you figure out what is causing your craving and help you find a solution. Here's what you can do about it, too:

Eat regular meals. Skipping meals just creates cravings. If you skip breakfast you'll feel starved by noon and crave JUNK FOODS.

Don't deprive yourself. No foods are always forbidden in SHAPEDOWN. Be sure to have your favorite food at least once a week.

Eat enough food. If your meals and snacks are too skimpy you'll get extra hungry and that hunger will fuel your cravings.

Eating secretly -- Kids who eat secretly usually feel badly about it. They take a cookie from the cupboard and "steal" some chips from the drawer. Eating secretly feels like you are lying. You feel like you've done something very wrong. It's not all your fault, though. Your parents' job is to make you feel comfortable talking with them about difficult things like wanting food that you're not supposed to have. It really doesn't matter whose fault it is. What matters is that from now on whenever you feel like eating secretly, you talk to your parents about it.

Your parents will help you with cravings and secretive eating in many different ways. One way they will help you is by making up trade-offs. Every once in a while when you really want something -- like an ice cream cone — they can help you figure out a way to eat less, eat lighter or exercise more the rest of the day so you can have it. Here are some examples of trade-offs:

> **Situation:** Matt wanted to go to a birthday party and eat the cake, ice cream, hot dog and chips.

> **Trade-off:** No dessert with dinner all week and two hours of exercise on the day of the party.

> **Situation:** Cindy wanted to have a candy bar for an after school snack.

> **Trade-off:** Half a sandwich and two baggies of veggies for lunch.

Eating style — What your family eats is your family nutrition. How they eat is your family eating style. There is an eating style that helps people enjoy their food more and feel more satisfied by their mealtimes. This eating style also helps them eat more healthfully.

A healthy family eating style is when parents and kids eat together at the same time and at the same table. Mealtime is about the same time every night. The television is off and nobody reads the newspaper. Everybody eats their food slowly and enjoys every bite. They talk about their feelings and say what's on their minds. They say what happened — both the good and the bad — in their lives that day. They don't talk about weight, eating, exercise or nutrition. They just enjoy the food they are eating. Parents don't urge the kids to eat or not to eat. Kids don't ask their parents how much they have to eat. This way of eating is good for both kids and parents and for both health and weight.

7

SMART TALK continued

Eating cues — Cravings can be triggered by cues like hunger, feeling deprived or sadness. We call anything that triggers you to say to yourself, "I want something to eat" an eating cue.

Hunger can be a cue but often cues have nothing to do with hunger. Often people, places, favorite foods, situations and moods trigger eating. If these non-hunger cues trigger your eating often, you're likely to gain weight. So keeping your weight down means learning how not to let non-hunger cues trigger you to eat. Here are some cues that trigger kids to eat:

Food — The smell of fresh, warm chocolate chip cookies as you walk through the mall, the sight of a juicy cheeseburger on a television commercial and the cookie jar, chocked full of sugar cookies calling to your across the kitchen are all cues to eat. Seeing, tasting, thinking about and feeling food can make you want to eat it, particularly when its food that you like.

People — It's difficult when Grandma bakes up your favorite brownies, when Dad brings home doughnuts or when your best friend hands you a chocolate candy bar. These people can trigger you to eat food you don't need.

Places — Places can trigger you to eat even though you really aren't hungry. The sight of the school snack bar or of the doughnut shop may signal you to eat. Simply being in the kitchen can trigger your thoughts to turn to food.

Situations — Certain situations like holiday feasts and birthday parties. Perhaps being home alone triggers you to eat or going to the mall with friends is difficult. Baby-sitting or having snacks after the baseball game may trigger you to eat more than you need. When you're sick you may eat non-stop, starting with hot chocolate and then working your way through the graham cracker box.

Moods — Almost any mood can be a cue to eat. Feeling angry, bored, tired, sad, anxious, happy, excited, frustrated, lonely, unloved, disgusted or guilty can prompt you to eat when you aren't really hungry.

Times — Certain times of the day can trigger you to eat. You may eat dinner just because it's dinner time or have a snack after school just because it's 3:30 p.m. You may eat just because it's time to eat.

Everybody gets these eating cues. If you eat when you get these cues, you'll probably always be heavy. But just the way that you have learned to eat when you get these cues, you can learn not to eat when you get them. Here are several strategies for stopping cues before they trigger you to eat.

Blocking — Stop the cue dead in it's tracks. Keep it from reaching you. Keep out of the kitchen and away from food. Tell people not to offer you food. Put space between yourself and food.

7

SMART TALK continued

Pausing—Instead of eating when you get the urge to eat, stop and figure out your choices. Decide to do one of them.

STEP 1. Pause

STEP 2. Think of all your choices (including eating)

STEP 3. List the good and bad about each choice

STEP 4. Decide on one choice and do it

At lunchtime at school Amy offered Cindy a cookie. She paused and thought of her choices: To say "No thanks!", to take it and eat it or to take it and save it for her grandpa. If she said "No thanks!" it would help her lose weight but she wouldn't get to eat the cookie. If she took the cookie and ate it she would enjoy the cookie right then, but later she would wish she hadn't. If she saved it for grandpa, he would eat it and it wouldn't be good for him either. Cindy thought of her choices and the good and bad of each and decided to say "No thanks!"

Delaying—You can put off eating. Just put off eating the food for ten minutes. Say to yourself, "If I still want the food in ten minutes, I'll eat it then." Lots of times at the end of ten minutes you don't want the food anymore.

As you figure out what your cues are and manage them you learn a lot about your feelings and how to control your eating. A lot of these skills can be used in other things that you do, too.

7

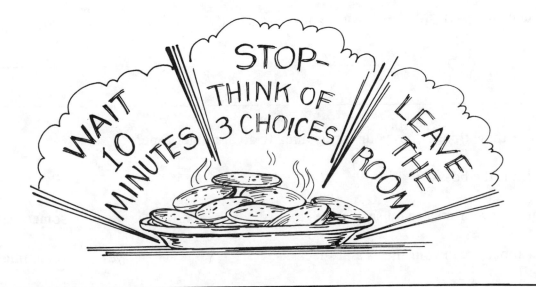

YOUR TURN!

1. Matt's cravings for candy were triggered by feeling deprived. Cindy's cues are watching TV, feeling sad and her grandpa's brownies. Both Cindy and Matt are working on their family's eating style. Name a food you've had a craving for:

_____

2. Why do you think you get cravings? (check all that are true for you):

_____ habit — I'm used to having that food

_____ deprived — having a too-healthy diet

_____ hunger — not eating enough

_____ feelings — like feeling sad, angry or bored

3. What will you do the next time you have a craving?

_____

_____

4. Name a food you've eaten secretly (without your mom or dad knowing).

_____

_____

5. What will you do the next time you want to eat secretly?

_____

_____

6. Which of these things does your family already do at dinner time?

Your parent is the boss of:

what time your meals and snacks are	yes	sometimes	no
what foods are in your meals and snacks	yes	sometimes	no

7

You are the boss of:

whether or not you eat	yes	sometimes	no
how much of the food you eat	yes	sometimes	no

Somebody reads books or newspapers when you are
eating with them.   yes   sometimes   no

You eat your food slowly, enjoying every bite.   yes   sometimes   no

You use Magic Words: "I feel", "I need",
"Would you Please"   yes   sometimes   no

7. What cues make you feel like eating when you really aren't hungry?

Feelings: happy   sad   lonely   angry   anxious   other_____

Times: after school   after dinner   weekends   other_____

People: friends   grandparents   neighbors   brother   sister

      mom   dad   other_____

Foods: favorite foods   fast foods   snack foods   other_____

Situations: parties   restaurants   birthdays   holidays   watching

      television   other_____

Places: kitchen   church   school   grandma's home   friend's home

      other_____

7

8. Name a cue that you get. What will you do when you get a cue?

Cue: _____

____ wait ten minutes before eating
____ stay out of the kitchen
____ stop and think of three choices
____ tell people not to offer me food
____ tell mom or dad that I feel like eating
____ other:_____

We took FAMILY TIME each day to review these records and to praise each other.

I watched no more than 0 2 4 6 8 hours of TV[1].

I EXERCISED[2] for 150 200 300 400 minutes or more.

I correctly filled out MY FOOD! on 4 or more days.

GOAL OF THE WEEK:
I told my parent one thing I like about myself on ___ or more days.

	MON.	TUES.	WED.	THURS.	FRI.	SAT.	SUN.	TOTAL	MET MY GOAL?
								___ days	YES / NO
								___ hours	YES / NO
								___ minutes	YES / NO
								___ days	YES / NO
								___ days	YES / NO

TOTAL NUMBER OF GOALS MET ⇒

[1] Hours per week of television:
0 = TV STAR 2 = NEWS ANCHOR 4 = GAME SHOW HOST 6 = WEATHER PERSON 8 = GAME SHOW RUNNER UP

[2] Minutes per week of exercise:
400 = STAR ATHLETE, 300 = IN SHAPE, 200 = GETTING STRONGER, 150 = GREAT START,

7

HOW TO USE: MY FOOD!

Now it is time to talk more about hunger - eating when you are hungry, stopping when you are just satisfied, not full. For the rest of SHAPEDOWN, you will fill out only two MY FOOD! records each week, but each time you start and stop eating, you will write how hungry or full you were. The code you will use is:

1 = very hungry

2 = hungry

3 = just satisfied

4 = full

5 = very full

This will help you pinpoint the times when you eat when you really are not hungry or stop eating when you are full. Whenever you start eating and really aren't hungry, ask yourself what has triggered you? Whenever you stop eating when you are stuffed, think about what triggered you to keep on eating.

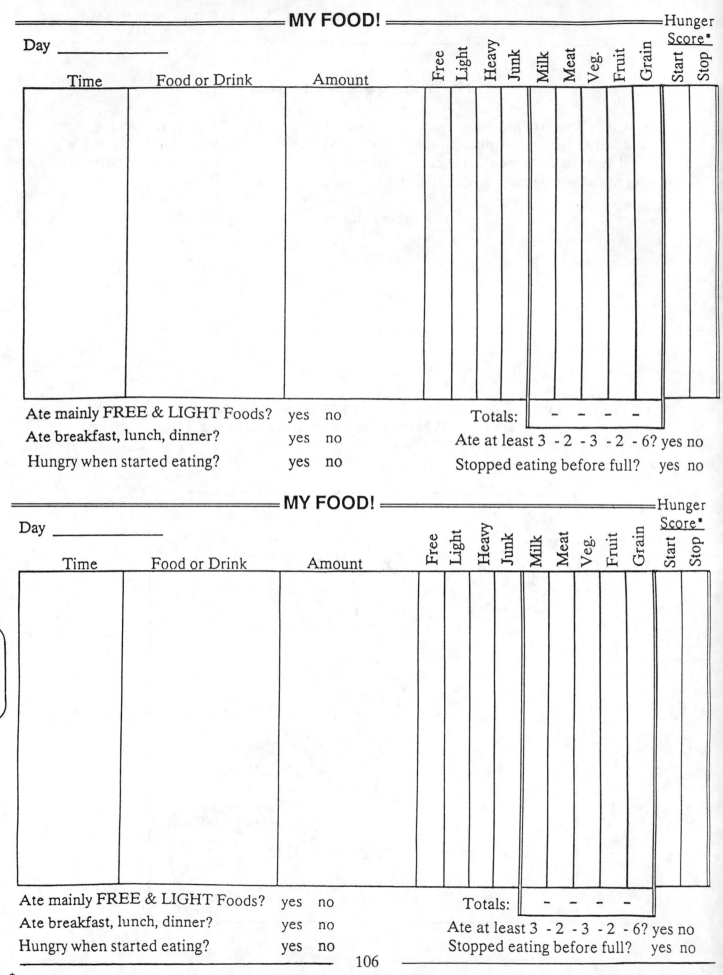

MY FOOD!

Day _____

Hunger Score*

Time	Food or Drink	Amount	Free	Light	Heavy	Junk	Milk	Meat	Veg.	Fruit	Grain	Start	Stop

Ate mainly **FREE & LIGHT** Foods? yes no

Ate breakfast, lunch, dinner? yes no

Hungry when started eating? yes no

Totals: – – – –

Ate at least 3 - 2 - 3 - 2 - 6? yes no

Stopped eating before full? yes no

MY FOOD!

Day _____

Hunger Score*

Time	Food or Drink	Amount	Free	Light	Heavy	Junk	Milk	Meat	Veg.	Fruit	Grain	Start	Stop

7

Ate mainly **FREE & LIGHT** Foods? yes no

Ate breakfast, lunch, dinner? yes no

Hungry when started eating? yes no

Totals: – – – –

Ate at least 3 - 2 - 3 - 2 - 6? yes no

Stopped eating before full? yes no

* 1 = very hungry, 2 = hungry, 3 = just satisfied, 4 = full, 5 = very full

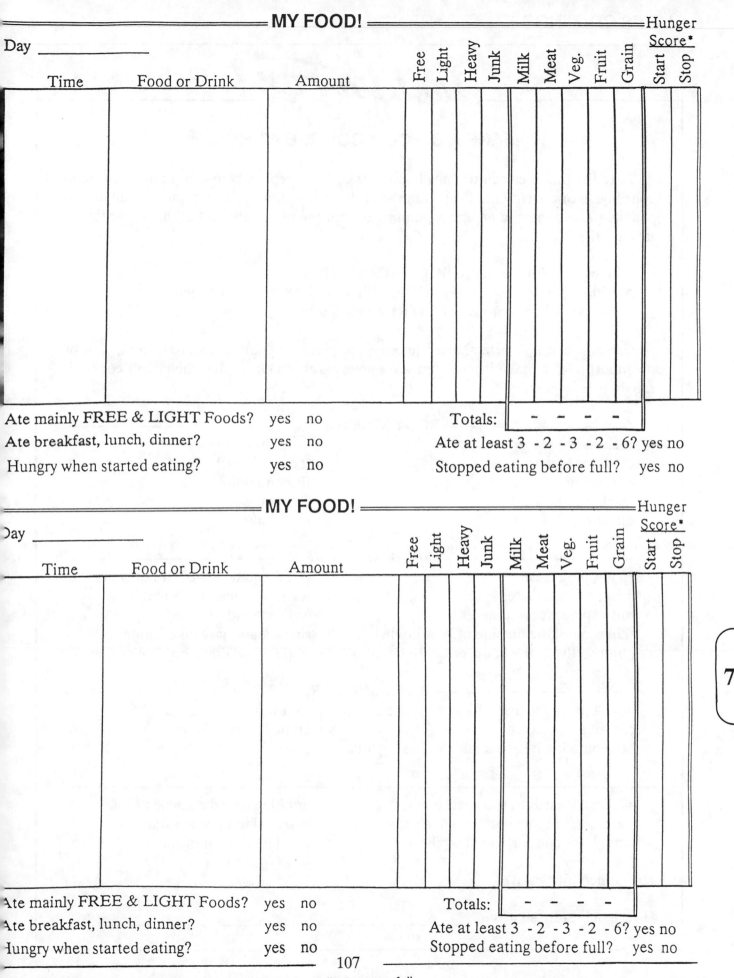

MY FOOD!

Day _____

Time	Food or Drink	Amount	Free	Light	Heavy	Junk	Milk	Meat	Veg.	Fruit	Grain	Hunger Score* Start	Stop

Ate mainly FREE & LIGHT Foods?　yes　no　　　　Totals: — — — —

Ate breakfast, lunch, dinner?　yes　no　　　　Ate at least 3 - 2 - 3 - 2 - 6? yes no

Hungry when started eating?　yes　no　　　　Stopped eating before full?　yes no

MY FOOD!

Day _____

Time	Food or Drink	Amount	Free	Light	Heavy	Junk	Milk	Meat	Veg.	Fruit	Grain	Hunger Score* Start	Stop

Ate mainly FREE & LIGHT Foods?　yes　no　　　　Totals: — — — —

Ate breakfast, lunch, dinner?　yes　no　　　　Ate at least 3 - 2 - 3 - 2 - 6? yes no

Hungry when started eating?　yes　no　　　　Stopped eating before full?　yes no

7

= very hungry, 2 = hungry, 3 = just satisfied, 4 = full, 5 = very full

Just for Fun!

MAKE A CIRCUIT COURSE AT HOME

Take the fun of circuit training home! Ask your parent to help you set up a course in your house or apartment. Post a note at each station. On each note, put a number, the activity to be done and an arrow pointing toward the next station. Let the whole family take part!

1. Start off with 3 or more BODY STRETCHES.
2. Move to 6 or more HUFF AND PUFF or BODY BUILDER activities.
3. End with 3 or more BODY STRETCHES activities.

Use music, props, prizes, and equipment or places in your garage, basement, yard or neighborhood to make it more fun. Ask your parent to check that the circuit course is safe before beginning.

BODY STRETCHES

neck rolls	knee lifts
shoulder shrugs	tuck and reach
arm swims	flex and point
reach for apples	foot rocks
sun circles	body hugs

HUFF AND PUFF

30 jumping jacks	go up and down a flight of stairs
dance for 5 minutes	jog to the neighbor's and back
run in place for 4 minutes	walk around the block
skip around the outside of your home	ride a stationary bike 2 miles
jump softly on the bouncer for 10 minutes	step up and down on a toilet seat

BODY BUILDERS

push-ups on the arm of an overstuffed chair	chin-ups
curl-ups	dumb bells
hold onto kitchen sink and do side leg lifts	

FUN

walk backwards to the next station	dribble around a kitchen chair
use a coffee table as a tunnel to crawl under	hop or skip between stations
jump back and forth over a pillow	crawl up a flight of stairs

How much fun was it? _____

How much exercise was it?_____

7

QUIZ #7

Directions: After you have read chapter 7, answer this practice quiz. Check your answers below. Then complete the final quiz. At your next session, you will check the answers to the final quiz.

TRUE OR FALSE

PRACTICE

__ 1. Skipping meals can cause cravings.

__ 2. If you eat secretly you should feel ashamed.

__ 3. When a child wants to eat secretly, he or she should tell a parent.

__ 4. The television should be off during dinner time.

__ 5. An example of blocking is not going into the kitchen so you won't see the box of cookies.

FINAL

__ 1. If you have a craving, tell your parent.

__ 2. Parents need to make kids feel comfortable telling them about wanting food.

__ 3. Parents and kids agree on trade-offs so children can eat the foods they want.

__ 4. Parents are in charge of the foods you can have for meals and snacks at home.

__ 5. An example of delaying is to put off eating for ten minutes.

Practice Quiz Answers: 1.T 2.F 3.T 4.T 5.T

8. CINDY'S AFTER SCHOOL ADVENTURE

Cindy sat in the cozy corner at the back of Ms. Bacon's class doing her math problems. She yawned. Math was boring and science dragged. She knew how to do everything there was to do on the playground. At home there was nothing worth doing but TV. She yawned again and quickly snapped her mouth closed as a fly buzzed past her nose. The fragrant spring air lazily drifted through the window rocking her to sleep.

Life was a little slow these days except for TV. In fact, life was boring. She thanked Mother Nature for the tube. Each afternoon she watched one favorite program after another. She wished that she could attach herself to the TV for good. Maybe a doctor could perform a complicated operation and then she'd never have to leave her beloved TV. Ever.

Matt was stuck on the third from the last math problem. He erased again. The paper shed little curls of paper. If he erased one more time he'd go clear through to the desk. Just then he caught a glimpse of Cindy, looking bored and restless. Cindy was looking leaner alright, but those bowls of candy cereal and the stacks of chocolate cookies she ate while watching the blaring tube didn't help.

Yoo hoo! Cindy! I miss you!

Cindy passed Matt a note, "Rescue me from this endless sea of boredom."

Matt chuckled and returned to the third to the last math problem.

Cindy passed another note, "Help, carry me to my television before I am snuffed out by the boredom monster."

Matt wrote, "Spend the afternoon with me and you'll ban boredom forever, that is, if you are brave enough!"

Matt slipped the note between the pages of his assignment book and tossed it onto Cindy's desk just as Ms. Bacon dropped her glasses on the floor and all the kids in the front row jumped up to retrieve them.

With a crooked smile on her expectant face, Cindy opened the assignment book and read Matt's challenge. Could she keep up with him all afternoon? Why not? Otherwise it would be the same old thing: television and candy cereal.

When the last bell rang, Cindy ran to find her backpack and raced up to Matt, "I'm ready," she said brightly, "but I'll bet you I'll be bored silly. My mind will wander to chocolate cookies and my candy cereal—the one with the little fruit flavored marshmallows in it."

Matt looked amused. "Just try not to be a slow poke!" he replied and hopped onto his bike. Cindy straddled her own and followed as Matt raced around the ivy-covered church and through the tunnel to the green lawn that stretched across the park. Matt jumped from his bike, grabbed a soccer ball and kicked it once, twice and then into the goal.

"One point for me," beamed Matt. "I'm going to beat you!"

"Wait! Stop!" said Cindy, putting the kick-stand down on her bike. The ball darted from her foot and the game was on.

When the score was four to four, Matt abruptly grabbed the ball and raced to his bike. "Beat you to my house!" he called.

His bike soared back through the tunnel, past the ivy-covered church, through the school yard and down the curvy street to his home with Cindy trailing all the way.

"Had enough?" Matt smiled.

"Never!" responded Cindy, her hair blowing in the wind and her cheeks flaming pink.

"Well, hold on!" he replied. Ralph, Matt's gray sheep dog sniffed at his heels. "It's bath time, my friend," said Matt and then grasped Ralph's collar, filled a tub with warm sudsy water and washed the dog until the water turned black and Ralph's white coat sparkled brightly.

Ralph emerged from the tub, looked straight into Cindy's eyes and shook. In one minute flat Cindy was soaked from head to food. She giggled. She laughed. She dropped to her knees, rolled on the grass and laughed some more. Ralph just licked her face.

Matt brought the wet towels into the house and found his mother's note. It read:

Matt,

Dinner tonight is fruit salad with vanilla yogurt and turkey sandwiches on whole wheat rolls. Will you pick up the freshest fruit and some non-fat yogurt at the store on your way home from karate class?

Thanks, Mom

P.S. Are we having foods from all Four Food Groups for dinner?

P.P.S. I love you.

8

Next to the note was a crisp ten dollar bill.

Just as Cindy peeked over Matt's shoulder to read the note, he tore out of the house and hopped on his bike. Cindy picked up the ten dollar bill, climbed onto her bike and raced after Matt down the curvy street to the karate school with all the mirrors on the walls.

For the next hour she watched the karate master moan, yell and strike. Matt moved smoothly and swiftly. She loved it. Cindy wanted to try. The karate master brought her to the middle of the mat and showed her one move. She tried it and felt silly. She tried it again and still felt silly. By the tenth time Cindy got it right! Matt smiled. The karate master smiled. Finally, Cindy smiled.

Back on their bikes, they felt the cooling afternoon air whirr past their ears. They darted down the street then stopped abruptly at the corner grocery store.

They picked out fruit, checking each apple, orange and banana for bad spots and ripeness. Cindy picked out two firm peaches and three tangerines. They looked for non-fat yogurt and couldn't see any.

Cindy walked up to the lady behind the counter with thick brown glasses covered with dirt from the day's work, "Do you have any non-fat yogurt?"

The woman raised her left eyebrow almost to the top of her forehead. "Little girl, it's all

8

non-fat yogurt. Can't you read?"

Cindy hung her head, slowly turned and walked to the back of the store. Now that she didn't get teased for being fat as much, she was being ridiculed for not reading. What luck!

Cindy said to Matt, who was reading the yogurt labels, "The checker lady with the brown glasses with two days worth of dirt on them says that they're all non-fat."

"Well," said Matt smugly, "some people don't know the difference between low-fat yogurt and non-fat yogurt."

Cindy smiled. She wasn't wrong after all. "Here's the non-fat yogurt, Matt, right on the bottom shelf! What kind do you want? Vanilla, peach or raspberry?"

"My Mom said vanilla, and she's the boss of the food we get, so let's get vanilla. I do like raspberry, so I'll ask her tonight during SHAPE-DOWN TIME if we could get raspberry next time."

Together Matt and Cindy marched up the aisle of the store with bags of fruit and cartons of vanilla non-fat yogurt, placed them on the counter and looked up at the checker lady. She quietly rang up their food — $6.15. Matt handed over the crisp ten dollar bill and she gave him back three quarters and three one dollar bills. He pocketed the change and picked up the brown paper bag brimming with fruit and yogurt.

"Wait!" said Cindy. The woman looked up sternly. "I mean, you owe us ten cents more, I think."

The woman's face softened. She took off her spotted, dusty glasses and said, "Pretty sharp, young lady. Here's your ten cents and an extra ten cents for being so alert."

Cindy blushed, clutched her two dimes and raced back to the bikes, not even noticing the racks of cookies and chips.

As Cindy and Matt slowly rode home, Cindy asked, "How'd I do, Matt?"

"You're a real champ, Cindy." he replied looking across his handlebars at her.

"I just wish my life was as exciting as yours. Can we trade lives, Matt, please?"

"Stick with your own life, Cindy. All we did was chores, exercise and interests. You can do that. You can start tomorrow. Just turn off the television. Pick out some things to do and do them!"

Cindy began to hum a sweet melody. Maybe she'd learn to play her grandpa's trumpet. Perhaps she'd ask her mom to sign her up for ballet lessons. Wouldn't it be fun to paint the fence in her front yard bright white? To race the vacuum around the downstairs rug? Her mind soared. Life was getting very, very exciting.

8

SMART TALK

Becoming active — Notice how your appetite changes? When you're doing something that's interesting and exciting, who cares about food? The hunger monster never knocks. Now, think again. What about when you come home from school to an empty house with nothing to do but homework? Microwaved pizza, chocolate chip cookies, even breakfast cereal and crackers beckon to you. Food surrounds you and convinces you that it's the only fun there is.

Food only helps hunger. It doesn't help you become stronger, smarter, more talented or better liked. Too much of it just makes you fatter. Television and food have one thing in common. They are both pacifiers. Imagine yourself with an oversized pacifier in your mouth every time you get hooked on television or food. Both television and food are good in small doses, but if they take up much time or attention they make a baby out of you.

So throw off those handcuffs of television and food and step into the world of activity. With activities you have to give a little more but you get a lot more back.

Think of a person stuck on television, food and school. That person grows up to be an adult who is stuck on television, food and work. Some life, huh? Now compare that to the life you can build if you start doing things, begin learning how to keep up a home by doing chores, develop talents and interests with classes and activities, and train your body by learning sports or dance. Bingo! You're an adult. Look at your life! It's as varied as a rainbow. Food and television are only a small part of the pleasure you get from your exciting and fun life.

What is an active lifestyle? That's simple. For most children it's doing at least an hour of exercise, half an hour of chores and half an hour of enriching activities every day.

With your new active lifestyle you'll be doing exercise, chores and other activities every day. You'll be more independent, walking and biking more and taking care of the house. Instead of being the child who can't do anything, you'll be a member of the family who really helps out. And the bonus for you is that you don't have time for that bowl of chips and that stack of cookies. Food is not on your mind! And you feel so proud of yourself. Your parents feel so proud of you, too. You're their active, healthy kid!

YOUR TURN!

Cindy and Matt have started getting active! Pick out some of the things you'd like to do for chores and interests that scare away the boredom monster!

1. Check all of the things you could do at home:

_____ make your own bed

_____ clean up your own room

_____ fold your own laundry and put it away

_____ set the table

_____ clear the table

_____ wash/rinse dishes

_____ clean out dishwasher or dry/put away dishes

_____ wipe off counters

_____ dust tabletops

_____ help make fruit or veggie salads for dinner

_____ cook simple dinners

_____ take out the trash

_____ get the mail

_____ feed the dog/cat

_____ groom the dog/cat

_____ sweep the garage

_____ pull weeds

_____ water plants

_____ sort laundry and put it in the washer and dryer

_____ clean bathroom sink and bathtub

_____ buy a few things at the convenience store

_____ sweep and mop the floors

_____ vacuum

_____ bathe the dog

_____ walk the dog

_____ other:_____

8

2. Check all of the activities that interest you:

_____ joining a sports team — like soccer

_____ taking a dance class — like ballet

_____ taking gymnastics classes

_____ learning to play tennis

_____ taking karate lessons

_____ learning to ski

_____ learning to skate

_____ arts and crafts

_____ collecting stamps

_____ looking at stars

_____ learning about space

_____ playing a musical instrument

_____ joining a choir

_____ going to the library

_____ taking drama lessons

_____ trying out for a play

_____ building things from wood

_____ sewing and needlework

_____ growing plants

_____ learning about animals

_____ starting a business

_____ doing volunteer work

3. What do you think will happen to you if you become more active?

_____ I won't feel bored as often.

_____ I will have more fun.

_____ I will learn how to do things.

_____ I will be more independent.

_____ I will eat less.

_____ I will not watch as much television.

_____ I will be happier.

_____ other_____

8

GIVE ME STROKES #8

	MON.	TUES.	WED.	THURS.	FRI.	SAT.	SUN.	TOTAL	MET MY GOAL?
We took FAMILY TIME each day to review these records and to praise each other.								___ days	YES NO
I watched no more than 0 2 4 6 8 hours of TV[1].								___ hours	YES NO
I EXERCISED[2] for 150 200 300 400 minutes or more.								___ minutes	YES NO
I correctly filled out MY FOOD! on 2 or more days.								___ days	YES NO
GOAL OF THE WEEK: Our family did chores together on ___ or more days.								___ days	YES NO

TOTAL NUMBER OF GOALS MET ⇒

[1] Hours per week of television:
0 = TV STAR 2 = NEWS ANCHOR 4 = GAME SHOW HOST 6 = WEATHER PERSON 8 = GAME SHOW RUNNER UP

[2] Minutes per week of exercise:
400 = STAR ATHLETE, 300 = IN SHAPE, 200 = GETTING STRONGER, 150 = GREAT START

117

8

Day _____

Time	Food or Drink	Amount	Free	Light	Heavy	Junk	Milk	Meat	Veg.	Fruit	Grain	Start	Stop

Hunger Score*

Ate mainly FREE & LIGHT Foods?   yes   no

Ate breakfast, lunch, dinner?   yes   no

Hungry when started eating?   yes   no

Totals: -   -   -   -

Ate at least 3 - 2 - 3 - 2 - 6? yes no

Stopped eating before full?   yes no

Day _____

Time	Food or Drink	Amount	Free	Light	Heavy	Junk	Milk	Meat	Veg.	Fruit	Grain	Start	Stop

Hunger Score*

8

Ate mainly FREE & LIGHT Foods?   yes   no

Ate breakfast, lunch, dinner?   yes   no

Hungry when started eating?   yes   no

Totals: -   -   -   -

Ate at least 3 - 2 - 3 - 2 - 6? yes no

Stopped eating before full?   yes no

* 1 = very hungry, 2 = hungry, 3 = just satisfied, 4 = full, 5 = very full

Just for Fun!

MAGIC GARDEN SOUP

Cook vegetables to make a magic soup. Where is the magic? In the vegetables. Watch how they change when you cook them!

Gather your materials

2 onions
6 celery stalks
4 carrots
3 tomatoes
3 other kinds of vegetables of your choice!
4 bouillon cubes
paring knife
large sauce pan or kettle

Make your soup

Wash the vegetables well, cut them in one inch slices and place them in a very large, deep pan. Add two quarts of warm water and 4 bouillon cubes plus any herbs you like, such as parsley, bay or basil. Cook over low heat until the vegetables are tender. Watch the vegetables change their texture and shape. Where did the tomatoes go to? For fun, about 10 minutes before it's done, add ½ cup alphabet noodles.

Enjoy your Magic Garden Soup

Ladle up your soup. You made the magic!

What three kinds of vegetables did you use?

_____

_____

_____

8

Just for Fun!

MIRROR BUDDY

Do you like your body and yourself better lately? If so, stand in front of a big mirror, in which you can see your whole body. See that person? That is your mirror buddy. Talk to your buddy.

1. Look at your buddy in the mirror. Tell your buddy three good things about him or her - like being kind, funny, friendly, nice, or smart, a good reader. What are they?

_____

_____

2. Keep on looking at your buddy. Tell your buddy three things that he or she has done to be proud of. What were they?

_____

_____

3. Look again in the mirror. Tell your buddy three things good about his or her body.

_____

_____

4. Now look at the mirror for the last time. Say something good and loving to your buddy, like "You are a good person," "I like you," or "You look good." Say it five times.

What did you say to yourself?_____

_____

How do you feel?_____

_____

8

QUIZ #8

Directions: After you have read chapter 8, answer this practice quiz. Check your answers below. Then complete the final quiz. At your next session, you will check the answers to the final quiz.

TRUE OR FALSE

PRACTICE

__ 1. Television for a child can act like a baby's pacifier.

__ 2. An active lifestyle for a child means doing 1/2 hour or more of chores per day.

__ 3. Children who don't do chores aren't as independent as children who do them.

__ 4. Children can mop and wax the kitchen floor.

__ 5. A child at 11 years of age can join a choir or grow carrots.

FINAL

__ 1. When people are busy, they don't think about food as much.

__ 2. An active lifestyle for a child includes 1/2 hour or more of hobbies or interests.

__ 3. Food and television should be only a small part of a person's pleasure in life.

__ 4. Children can fold their own laundry and put it away.

__ 5. A child at 11 years of age can learn to paint a bedroom.

Practice Quiz Answers: 1.T 2.T 3.T 4.T 5.T

8

9. AMY LEARNS A LESSON

Tomorrow would be Jesse's birthday. The other three kids in the cozy corner of Ms. Bacon's class were planning a party for him. Everybody knew about it, that is, except Jesse. Amy, Cindy and Matt had invited the whole class to meet right after school near the tall trees next to the library for the party.

Ms. Baker knew about it and said that she would bring the plates, cups, table cloths and napkins. She even said that she would bring her baby birds to class that day to add to the festivities! Sophia at the office knew, too. She said she'd hope for clear skies and bright sunshine for that afternoon.

With only one day to go Amy, Cindy and Matt gathered together at the corner table in the lunch area to plan the party.

"Let's play soccer," suggested Cindy.

"Good idea! That's Jesse's favorite sport!" responded Matt.

"What about music?" asked Cindy.

"I know. I'll bring my tape player," volunteered Amy.

"And I'll bring my tapes," said both Matt and Cindy in unison.

"Great!" replied Amy.

There was silence.

"Ummm. What about food, Matt?" asked Cindy.

"Why, of course, we'll have chocolate fudge cake topped with miniature marshmallows. It's my favorite," interrupted Amy.

Matt looked at Cindy. Cindy looked at Matt.

Slowly Matt said, "Good idea, Amy. Why don't you bring that since it's your favorite?"

Cindy continued, "But not everybody wants to eat greasy, gooey cake so I'll bring a fruit salad."

"And I'll bring a plate of veggies with my favorite dip," said Matt.

"Veggies? Who wants to eat veggies at a party? This is supposed to be fun, you know," snarled Amy.

Matt snickered softly and turned to Amy, "I'm sure, Amy, that we can all have fun whether we're stuffing our faces with gooey chocolate marshmallow cake, crunching on crisp veggies or slurping up mounds of cut-up fruit. The party and the people are the fun, not the goop!"

Cindy winked at Matt. If only Clown could see Matt now!

"Remember Valentine's Day, Amy?" said Cindy.

"Sure I do. I had the flu and my dad brought me a huge red heart with chocolate and marsh-mallow creams in it."

"Did the creams make your Valentine's Day happy?" probed Matt.

"My Valentine's Day wasn't very happy anyway. My nose was drippy and my head ached. I almost had to go to the doctor's."

"What about the creams?" asked Cindy.

"They were pretty, but they didn't taste very good. They were under my bed until last week when an army of ants got them." Amy explained.

"For Valentine's Day my mom gave me a mystery book for my collection and my grandpa gave me a red rose. We all went to a movie together," said Cindy.

"We had fun, too," added Matt. "Mom and dad gave me a new football and we played football at school with our neighbor. It was crisp and cold but we ran so much that we were sweating! It was a great day!"

"You guys are making me feel dumb," said Amy, pouting.

"We're not making you feel any way. Besides, how can you feel dumb when you have the best math grades in the whole class? We're just telling you how we celebrate holidays and parties. We don't pig out," said Matt.

"Okay," challenged Amy, "you don't pig out at birthday parties or Valentine's Day, but what about Halloween and Christmas? I bet you crawl on your knees to get candy and cookies then!"

Cindy smiled at her friend and gently put her arm around her, "No, Amy, the fun of Halloween is the costumes and the parties. I'll still get

9

some candy this year, but I probably won't eat much of it."

Matt added, "The holidays may be a little harder, but even if I'm surrounded by cookies, I eat some of them but I won't stuff them in."

Amy raised her eyebrow, "You won't? How come? Is it because you can't because you're still a little chunky?"

"That's not it. Some of that stuff is okay even when I'm losing weight. It's just that I don't crave it any more. I can get it when I want it and that's enough. I don't eat a lot of candy and cookies because I've stopped wanting them. I'm more interested in things other than eating."

"I bet you don't have six cavities every year when you go to the dentist like I do," sighed Amy.

Matt and Cindy smiled and Cindy turned to Amy, "One year I had 10 cavities. This year I'm shooting for none!"

The next day was Jesse's party. Sophia's wishes paid off. The day was bright and sunny with a light breeze that lifted the spirits. Ms. Bacon brought her birds and the kids peeked at them one at a time. Ms. Bacon said that the birds were very sensitive and couldn't tolerate too much noise and stimulation. She gave the biggest baby bird to Jesse for his birthday. He could pick it up as soon as the baby bird was ready to leave his mother.

9

When the last bell rang at school, all the kids in Ms. Bacon's class, including all four children in the cozy corner, sprang for the door and raced to the grove of trees next to the library. Out of the backpacks sprang party food. Cindy brought cut up pears, peaches, apples, oranges and pineapple. Matt uncovered a huge tray of carrots, celery, cucumbers, broccoli and radishes all cut up, and two bowls of dip. They laid them all out on the tablecloth that Ms. Bacon had brought.

Where was Amy's chocolate fudge cake with miniature marshmallows on top? In fact, where was Amy? Cindy and Matt looked all around.

"There she is!" shouted Matt, "over there, coming from the office." Amy walked toward them carrying a large platter covered with a cloth. She took each step carefully. All the kids began to gather around the tablecloth, helping themselves to veggies and fruit and waiting for Amy to unveil her cake.

Amy walked up to the group and gently placed the platter in the middle of the tablecloth. It was warm. It smelled wonderful and fresh.

"Jesse," called Cindy, "come quickly!"

Jesse raced to the tablecloth and fell to his knees. Amy smiled at him and lifted the cloth.

Fresh bread! Fragrant, soft whole wheat bread! Five loaves of it with candles stuck in each—11 candles altogether.

"Bread?" said David.

"Bread?" said Jesse.

"That's right, it's bread!" said Amy.

Just then the aroma of the fresh bread swirled around them and Cindy threw her head back, breathed in and said, "Ohhhhhh! It smells so wonderful!"

"Mmmmm," said David, "It smells almost as good as cake."

Amy gloated and turned as Sophia began cutting the fresh bread, "I brought the dough to school and Sophia helped me bake it in the school oven."

Jesse reached for a piece of bread and bit into a soft fragrant slice still warm from the oven. "It's not cake, but it's delicious!"

The rest of the kids from Ms. Bacon's room 6 each grabbed a piece of bread and took off for the soccer field. Later, after the birthday songs had been sung, the veggies crunched, the fruit salad slurped, the bread munched, and the tablecloths, plates and napkins cleaned up, Cindy and Matt talked as they slowly walked home. They had joined their SHAPEDOWN CLUB 10 weeks ago. The group was winding down, even though they would go see the group leader every so often.

Cindy felt sad. "I'm going to miss the kids in the group, Matt, especially Kristin and Michael."

"And I'm going to miss Jason and Ben. I wish they went to our school," said Matt.

"Yes, but we can still be SHAPEDOWN buddies, can't we?" asked Cindy.

"Of course we can, Cindy," replied Matt. "Plus we have another special friend to count on."

"Me?" questioned Clown appearing on the stone wall next to the sidewalk.

Cindy laughed, "Clown, I've been meaning to give you a hug!" and she reached over to give

9

him a very warm hug with her not so round, not so soft and not so fluffy body.

Matt stayed back. "Clown," he said seriously, "You've helped me a lot, too. See my body? It's a little leaner. And I've stopped stuffing and starving. I have a ways to go until I need smaller pants, but I'm getting there!"

Cindy let Clown out of her warm embrace, "And you've helped me talk about my feelings and stand up for myself. Sure I'm getting leaner, but I'm also happier and busier. I don't even have much time for television anymore." Cindy turned to Matt, "And you, too, my buddy. You've helped me every step of the way."

Matt smiled, "We've been good buddies for each other, alright, but I'm worried I won't keep it up!"

Clown stepped forward, his suit filled out with muscles and vitality, "I'm not worried much. Ups and downs are normal. When my eating and exercise aren't healthy, it's no big deal. I haven't blown it. I've just taken a little vacation from healthy habits. I'm just going to get right back on track."

"That's right, Matt," laughed Cindy. "Plus we can keep up our SHAPEDOWN CLUB. There is a new advanced SHAPEDOWN for kids like us that have graduated from SHAPEDOWN. I'm going to talk to my grandpa about it."

Cindy turned on her heels and with a wink and a smile shouted, "Hey, you two, race you to my house!"

Matt and Cindy raced down the street and streaked around the corner. Clown disappeared from the rock wall and reappeared on the counter in Cindy's kitchen. Like magic he folded up his legs, making himself into a cookie jar once again. He heard the door bang as Cindy and Matt came running in, still laughing. There was a little bit of magic in the air that didn't come from Clown. It came from two other smart people, Matt and Cindy.

9

SMART TALK

Special occasions—Birthdays, Valentine's Day, Halloween, Christmas or Hanukkah, Easter, and Thanksgiving are festive times. They usually mean JUNK FOOD. But eating is only part of the fun. You can have a great time without overeating. What can you do to make special occasions fun yet healthy?

Ask your mom and dad to stop giving you food gifts. Tell them you want flowers, money, books, toys or anything else that isn't food.

If you get food gifts, give them away. Food gifts are fun to look at and play with, but they won't help you become leaner and fitter. If you like, have a taste or two, then give it away.

Ask your mom and dad to serve more veggies, fruits and other lighter foods for holidays and parties.

Praise your mom and dad when they serve lighter foods or give you things other than food. Moms and dads like praise, too.

Before a party, during FAMILY TIME try to plan what you will eat at the party. If you want to eat sweet or fatty foods, plan trade-offs so that parties don't stop you from losing weight.

Speak up and say "no thanks" when food you didn't plan to eat is offered to you.

Keep in mind that the fun of parties is mainly the people and activities—not the food. Halloween is fun because you have costumes, parties and trick or treating. You also get to sort and play with the candy. Is eating the candy really the best part of the holiday? Most kids say "NO!"

You have done well! In the last few weeks you have made some changes in your food and exercise. You have probably made some changes in your fitness and weight, too. You know more about nutrition, exercise and communication. Chances are your family has made some healthy changes, too.

9

SMART TALK continued

This part of SHAPEDOWN is coming to an end. You can plan what kind of help you want during the coming weeks to keep up the healthy habits you have started in SHAPEDOWN.

Most families continue to get help by joining ADVANCED SHAPEDOWN. In ADVANCED SHAPEDOWN you continue to get lots of ideas and help on how to continue to lose weight and ways to keep if off. Some families see their SHAPEDOWN group leader for visits every few weeks or once a month. You and your family can still keep track of your weight by weighing once a week and support each other by taking FAMILY TIME, too. Some families get other kinds of counseling like help with how the family or the parents get along. Others want no additional support and go it on their own.

The changes you have started in SHAPEDOWN will not disappear. They are not magic. They are better than magic. They are real. You have learned to talk about your feelings and needs, to eat in a healthy way, and to enjoy exercise more. You have made these changes. Nobody made them for you. Now it's your job to continue them. When the going gets tough, it's your job to ask for some help from your parent or group leader.

When you get off track and stop exercising and eating well, it's not the end of the world. You're just taking a little vacation from healthy habits. The trick is to get back to exercising and eating well right away.

Thanks for being part of SHAPEDOWN. It's not easy to have a weight problem as a kid. But there are some good things about it. You can use the ideas you learned in SHAPEDOWN with lots of problems — not just weight. So you have a head start on other kids in knowing how to handle difficulties like a pro.

You've also helped your family shape up their food and exercise. We hope SHAPEDOWN has helped them feel healthier and closer and that it has given you the boost you needed to put weight problems behind you and get on with a more fun and active life.

9

YOUR TURN!

1. Cindy has started getting her party fun from people, not food. Matt has asked his mom to stop giving him candy gifts. Name one fun thing that doesn't involve food about each of these special occasions.

Valentine's Day _____

Halloween _____

Thanksgiving _____

Christmas/Hanukkah _____

Birthday parties _____

2. List the special occasions or holidays for which your parents or other people give you food gifts (candy and other sweets).

the occasion	the food they give me
_____	_____
_____	_____
_____	_____

3. Ask your parents or these other people to stop giving you food gifts. Tell them what gifts you would like instead of food. Check the gifts you would like:

____ flowers   ____ movie tickets

____ books   ____ a friend overnight

____ games   ____ a new toy

____ balls   ____ clothes

____ money   ____ jewelry

____ family outing   ____ other things_____

____ an outing with a friend

9

4. Ask your Mom and Dad to serve lighter foods for special occasions and holidays. Check the foods you'd like them to serve as part of special occasion meals:

_____ veggies and dip   _____ light ice cream

_____ bread sticks   _____ sugar-free sodas

_____ fresh fruit salad   _____ mineral water and fruit juice

_____ crisp salads   _____ veggies without fat

_____ bread without butter   _____ rice or potatoes without fat

_____ fruit desserts

5. Which of these changes did you make in SHAPEDOWN?

_____ know more about food and exercise   _____ do more chores

_____ talk about my feelings more   _____ communicate better with my parents

_____ speak up about my needs and prob-   _____ family feels closer
      lems more
                                           _____ feel better about my body
_____ exercise more
                                           _____ feel better about me
_____ eat more regular meals
                                           _____ am stronger
_____ eat more LIGHT FOODS and
      FREE FOODS   _____ family is more organized

_____ eat less   _____ can run farther before I get tired

_____ am more active after school   _____ lost weight

_____ have more interests and activities   _____ other_____

6. List the three changes of which you are proudest:

1._____

2._____

3._____

9

7. List some changes that you have not made. For instance, perhaps it's still difficult for you to talk about your feelings.

1. _____

2. _____

3. _____

8. What are your goals for the next three months?

I will lose weight: _____ pounds

I will exercise more: _____ minutes

                       _____ days per week

                       Kinds of exercise: _____

_____

_____

I will eat more healthfully: _____ eat more **FREE FOODS and LIGHT FOODS**

                       _____ eat regular meals

                       _____ eat less

                       _____ eat when I'm hungry

                       _____ stop before I am full

I will speak up more: _____ about my feelings

                       _____ about my needs

                       _____ to ask for what I need

I will feel better: _____ about myself

                       _____ about my body

9

Other goals: _____

_____

_____

9. What kinds of help do you want in the next three months?

_____ begin ADVANCED SHAPEDOWN

_____ visits with our SHAPEDOWN instructor

_____ get referral for other kinds of help

_____ go it alone

Thank you!

_____

GIVE ME STROKES #9

	MON.	TUES.	WED.	THURS.	FRI.	SAT.	SUN.	TOTAL	MET MY GOAL?
We took FAMILY TIME each day to review these records and to praise each other.								____ days	YES / NO
I watched no more than 0 2 4 6 8 hours of TV[1].								____ hours	YES / NO
I EXERCISED[2] for 150 200 300 400 minutes or more.								____ minutes	YES / NO
I correctly filled out MY FOOD! on 2 or more days.								____ days	YES / NO
GOAL OF THE WEEK: Our family ate dinner together on ____ or more days.								____ days	YES / NO

133

TOTAL NUMBER OF GOALS MET ⇒

[1] Hours per week of television:
0 = TV STAR 2 = NEWS ANCHOR 4 = GAME SHOW HOST 6 = WEATHER PERSON 8 = GAME SHOW RUNNER UP

[2] Minutes per week of exercise:
400 = STAR ATHLETE, 300 = IN SHAPE, 200 = GETTING STRONGER, 150 = GREAT START

═══════════════════════ **MY FOOD!** ═══════════════════════ Hunger Score*

Day _____

Time	Food or Drink	Amount	Free	Light	Heavy	Junk	Milk	Meat	Veg.	Fruit	Grain	Start	Stop

Ate mainly **FREE & LIGHT** Foods?   yes   no   Totals: –   –   –   –

Ate breakfast, lunch, dinner?   yes   no   Ate at least 3 - 2 - 3 - 2 - 6? yes no

Hungry when started eating?   yes   no   Stopped eating before full?   yes no

═══════════════════════ **MY FOOD!** ═══════════════════════ Hunger Score*

Day _____

Time	Food or Drink	Amount	Free	Light	Heavy	Junk	Milk	Meat	Veg.	Fruit	Grain	Start	Stop

Ate mainly **FREE & LIGHT** Foods?   yes   no   Totals: –   –   –   –

Ate breakfast, lunch, dinner?   yes   no   Ate at least 3 - 2 - 3 - 2 - 6? yes no

Hungry when started eating?   yes   no   Stopped eating before full?   yes no

9

* 1 = very hungry, 2 = hungry, 3 = just satisfied, 4 = full, 5 = very full

MAKE A PIZZA !

It's pizza time! Let's make pizza that is a LIGHT FOOD and will tickle your taste buds! Make it on your own or with your family. Get an OK to use the oven from your parent.

Gather these foods:

> frozen whole wheat bread dough
> a jar of pizza sauce
> low fat mozzarella cheese
> two or more veggies like mushrooms, green peppers, onions, green onions, zucchini, garlic, and tomatoes

Early in the day:

> take bread dough out of the freezer
> grate mozzarella cheese
> chop or slice 2 cups of vegetables

One hour before serving:

> preheat oven to 375 degrees
> punch down dough with your fist
> roll dough out on a floured board to form a large circle
>
> place dough on a non-stick cookie tray
> top with pizza sauce, cheese and veggies
> cover with a paper towel, put in a warm place for 20 minutes
> bake for 20 to 30 minutes or until browned and bubbling.

Enjoy your pizza!

With which vegetables did you top your pizza?

_____

How did your pizza taste?

_____

9

QUIZ #9

Directions: After you have read chapter 9, answer this practice quiz. Check your answers below. Then complete the final quiz. At your next session, you will check the answers to the final quiz.

TRUE OR FALSE

PRACTICE

__ 1. A person has no choice but to eat lots of JUNK FOOD on Halloween.

__ 2. SHAPEDOWN recommends that you tell people that you don't want food gifts.

__ 3. When you eat dinner at someone's house, it's rude to say "no, thanks" to dessert.

__ 4. You should definitely have some candy on Valentines Day, if you feel deprived.

__ 5. SHAPEDOWN stops after this session and you are completely on your own.

FINAL

__ 1. A person can still have fun on holidays even if they don't overeat.

__ 2. If someone gives you candy for a gift, you have to eat it.

__ 3. To make a holiday healthy, plan some family exercise.

__ 4. It is better to have a piece of pumpkin pie than to have none and feel deprived.

__ 5. Most families go on to ADVANCED SHAPEDOWN to lose more weight and to help keep it off.

Practice Quiz Answers: 1.F 2.T 3.F 4.T 5.F

9

MY WEIGHT RECORD

Write down your starting weight. This weight corresponds to the "0" at the black dot under week 1. Compare your weight each week with your starting weight. For example, if your starting weight was 162 pounds and your weight at week 2 was 161 pounds, you should put a dot at -1 under week 2. Then connect the two dots. Continue plotting like this each week.

MY STARTING WEIGHT: _____

MY ENDING WEIGHT: _____

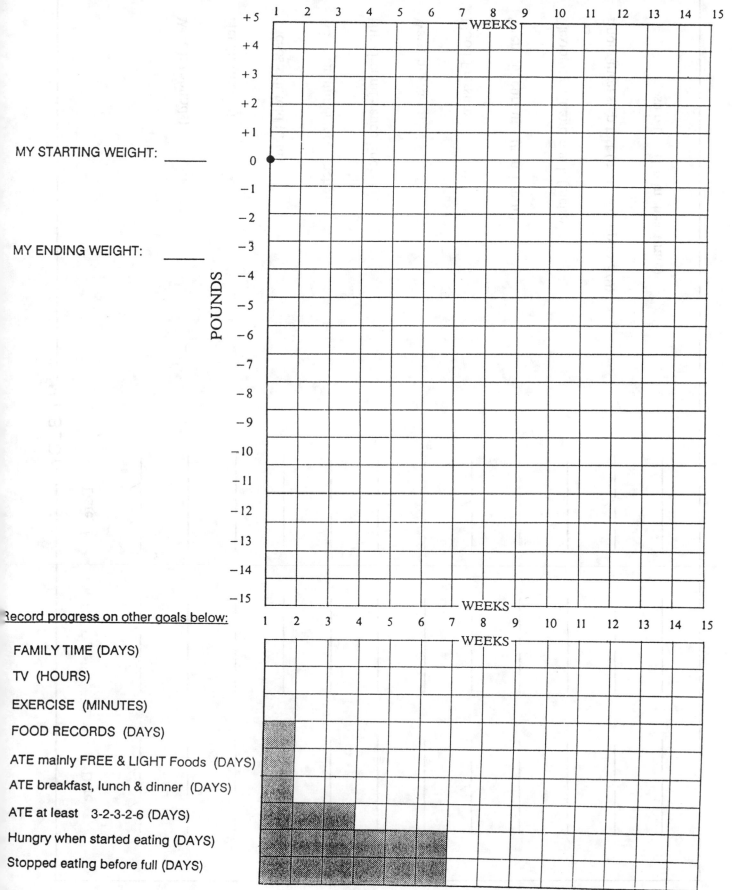

Record progress on other goals below:

FAMILY TIME (DAYS)

TV (HOURS)

EXERCISE (MINUTES)

FOOD RECORDS (DAYS)

ATE mainly FREE & LIGHT Foods (DAYS)

ATE breakfast, lunch & dinner (DAYS)

ATE at least 3-2-3-2-6 (DAYS)

Hungry when started eating (DAYS)

Stopped eating before full (DAYS)

137

MY BODY

	Date	Date	Date
Weight (pounds)	___	___	___
Height (inches)	___	___	___
Triceps skinfold (mm)	___	___	___
Waist circumference (inches)	___	___	___
Hip circumference (inches)	___	___	___
Waist:hip ratio	___	___	___
Blood Pressure	__/__	__/__	__/__
Strength: curl-ups (# in 1 min.)	___	___	___
Flexibility: sit and reach (inches)	___	___	___
Endurance: step test (min./sec. up to 3/0)	__/__	__/__	__/__
step test (1 min. heart rate)	___	___	___

138

FOOD SUMMARY

FREE FOODS	artichokes asparagus bamboo shoots broccoli brussels sprouts cabbage carrots cauliflower celery cucumbers eggplant green beans green onions	greens jicama lettuce mushrooms onions peppers radishes sauerkraut sour pickles dill pickles sprouts summer squash tomatoes	water chestnuts zucchini water mineral water diet soda soda water tea coffee broth tomato juice vegetable juice limes lemons	plain popcorn tabasco sauce soy sauce horseradish garlic onion powder cinnamon herbs spices flavorings mustard vinegar no-oil salad dressing

LIGHT FOODS	non-fat milk
	low-fat milk (1%)
	non-fat buttermilk
	reduced fat cheese
	low-fat cottage
	  cheese
	plain low-fat
	  yogurt
	dried beans
	split peas
	black-eyed peas
	lentils
	refried beans
	turkey, light
	  meat, no skin
	chicken, light
	  meat, no skin
		fish
		tuna, canned
		  in water
		lean red meat,
		  all fat removed
		apples
		applesauce, canned
		  without sugar
		apricots
		bananas
		blackberries
		cantaloupe
		cherries
		grapefruit
		grapes
		nectarines
		oranges
			papaya
			pineapple
			peaches
			plums
			raisins
			prunes
			strawberries
			tangerines
			watermelons
			fruit, canned
			  in water
			fruit, canned
			  in juice
			potatoes
			sweet potatoes
			peas
			winter squash
				clear soups
				vegetable soups
				bread
				bagel
				biscuits
				english muffins
				hamburger buns
				low-fat crackers
				unsweetened cereal
				hominy grits
				tortillas
				plain spaghetti
				rice cakes
				rice
				bran
				barley
				bulgar

HEAVY FOODS	low-fat milk (2%)
	whole milk
	chocolate milk
	cheese
	creamed cottage
	  cheese
	flavored yogurt
	ice milk
	low-fat frozen
	  yogurt
	pudding
	tofu
	peanuts
	peanut butter
		almonds
		sunflower seeds
		chicken or turkey
		  with skin
		chicken or turkey
		  dark meat
		fried chicken
		turkey hot dogs
		fish sticks
		fried fish
		tuna, packed in
		  oil
		red meat
		eggs
			cream soups
			macaroni &
			  cheese
			macaroni salad
			potato salad
			pizza
			chili
			avocado
			sauced vegetables
			fruit rolls
			sweetened
			  applesauce
			fruit, canned
			  in syrup
				coconut
				fries
				hash browns
				sweetened cereals
				granola
				high-fat crackers
				taco shells
				stuffing
				corn bread
				muffins
				pancakes
				waffles
				french toast
				buttered popcorn

JUNK FOODS	ice cream sherbet shakes cream cheese sour cream half and half whipped cream cream sauce bacon sausage hot dogs salami salt pork	fruit drinks kool-aid jello chips pies cakes cookies doughnuts pastries croissants candy cereal granola candy bars	candy chocolate chocolate topping syrup honey jam jelly marmalade sugar popsicles regular sodas sweet pickles gum	beer wine liquor butter margarine oil lard gravy mayonnaise tartar sauce salad dressing olives salt

I want to share SHAPEDOWN with the person named below. Please:

____ send this person the SHAPEDOWN parent guide and child'or teen workbook I've ordered below and the names and addresses of the three SHAPEDOWN programs nearest to him or her. (Complete order form below.)

____ send this person complete SHAPEDOWN information and the names and addresses of the three SHAPEDOWN programs nearest to him or her.

_____ CONSIDER ADVANCED SHAPEDOWN _____

____ send me a copy of ADVANCED SHAPEDOWN.

ADVANCED SHAPEDOWN is for all SHAPEDOWN families to support the changes made in SHAPEDOWN in becoming permanent. The guide is a helping hand that stimulates you to keep on track, further sharpen your skills in food, exercise and communication and prepares you for the changing needs of the adolescent. For your copy of the ADVANCED SHAPEDOWN Guide, check with your SHAPEDOWN instructor or use this form to order directly from the publisher.

_____ ORDER FORM _____

Quantity	Item #	Description	Cost	Amount
_____	451	SHAPEDOWN - Level 1 Workbook (Ages 6 to 8)	18.95	_____
_____	452	SHAPEDOWN - Level 2 Workbook (Ages 9 or 10)	18.95	_____
_____	454	SHAPEDOWN - Level 3 Workbook (Ages 11 or 12)	18.95	_____
_____	453	SHAPEDOWN Parent's Guide To Supporting Your Child	18.95	_____
_____	457	ADVANCED SHAPEDOWN Children's Workbook	18.95	_____
_____	459	ADVANCED SHAPEDOWN Child's Parent Guide	18.95	_____
_____	401	SHAPEDOWN Just For Teens! Workbook (ages 12-20)	18.95	_____
_____	402	SHAPEDOWN Parent's Guide To Supporting Your Teen	18.95	_____
_____		Shipping per book	3.00	_____
			TOTAL	_____

Payment method: ▢ Visa/Mastercard # _____ Exp. ___/___.

▢ Check (payable to BALBOA PUBLISHING)

SHIP   Name _____
TO:

Address _____

City _____ State _____ Zip _____

Please mail your order to:

BALBOA PUBLISHING
1323 San Anselmo Avenue
San Anselmo, CA 94960

Or you may order on the Internet: **www.shapedown.com**

Or phone (**415-453-8886**), fax (**415-453-8888**), or email (**shapedown@aol.com**)your order.